D0410710

A SLOW BOAT TO
HONG KONG

Also by Marianne MacKinnon:

The Naked Years

The Alien Years

The Deluge

The Quarry

Reflections

SC 9/19

A SLOW BOAT TO HONG KONG

Marianne MacKinnon

sc 1/14

Book Guild Publishing
Sussex, England

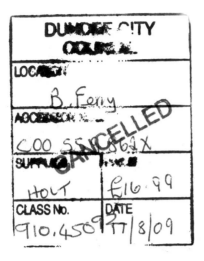

DUNDEE CITY
COUNCIL

LOCATION
B. Ferry

ACCESSION
C00 559 862 X

SUPPLIER
HOLT   £16.99

CLASS No.   DATE
910.450   17/8/09

CANCELLED

First published in Great Britain in 2009 by
The Book Guild Ltd
Pavilion View
19 New Road
Brighton, BN1 1UF

Copyright © Marianne MacKinnon 2009

The right of Marianne MacKinnon to be identified as the author
of this work has been asserted by her in accordance with the
Copyright, Designs and Patents Act 1988.

All rights reserved. No part of this publication may be
reproduced, transmitted, or stored in a retrieval system, in any
form or by any means, without permission in writing from the
publisher, nor be otherwise circulated in any form of binding or
cover other than that in which it is published and without a
similar condition being imposed on the subsequent purchaser.

Typesetting in Times by
Keyboard Services, Luton, Bedfordshire

Printed and bound in Great Britain by
CPI Antony Rowe

A catalogue record for this book is available from
The British Library

ISBN 978 1 84624 288 5

For my sons

*Wenn einer eine Reise tut,
so kann er was erzählen…*

Matthias Claudius

Contents

PART III   A Jinxed Homeward Passage

Foreword

The passage to Hong Kong on a cargo vessel in June 1961 with three small children, and the return voyage on the P&O liner SS *Oronsay* on 26 June 1967, form a major package of my memories of the sixties, as do cameo-like episodes from our expatriate years in the former Crown Colony, when the handover to China in 1997 was not yet an emotive subject.

Although many of my friends who once lived there have since paid return visits, I have never been back, either as a tourist or in order to do background research for this book. For the Hong Kong I knew is no longer. Red flags with five stars now dominate the cityscape. Development, I am told, has taken place on a massive scale, both on Hong Kong Island and on the mainland. The new out-of-town airport will no doubt have been welcomed by pilots who, on their approach to and take-off from the former strip at Kai Tak, had to sweep so low over adjacent Kowloon City that each time planes threatened to shave off the roofs of this densely populated area. At least one serious accident demonstrated the risk to passengers and residents at the time, when a BOAC aircraft overshot the narrow landing strip and crashed into the Bay. Also, I hear, more land has been reclaimed from the sea and a new two-lane tunnel now connects Kowloon with Hong Kong island. The former red pillar boxes are now painted a 'Chinese green', and Hong Kong's banknotes no longer feature the Queen – minor changes with which Peking (now Beijing) has subtly tried to decolonise the former British territory. In Kowloon's hinterland, the New Territories, satellite towns have risen in places which I remember as being lush and vibrant with monkeys and wildlife, and whole hillsides and tracts of subtropical jungle – once familiar walking territory – have had to make way for new building schemes.

In the light of all this I felt that, if I had visited Hong Kong as a former expatriate, its changed face and political complexion would have superimposed themselves on my mind, blurring the true features of my recollections. I have, therefore, restricted myself to narrating personal experiences of the humorous, poignant or pivotal kind. This is, therefore, not a travelogue in the accepted sense, but a memoir in which an 'outer' journey through some of the world's most extraordinary places goes hand in hand with an 'inner' journey towards personal enlightenment and maturity.

Voyaging by cargo boat has always held a special attraction for those who like an informal, more intimate form of sea travel and the chance to visit ports around the world at which ocean liners do not call. In the early sixties, a British cargo vessel bound for the Far East might take up to twelve passengers on board. Small they might be but the one-class bunk-bedded cabins often came with postage stamp-sized private facilities. When sailing through hot climes, passengers could cool down in a canvas seawater pool on the foredeck and, if sleepless in oven-like cabins, join the night on deckchairs. Freighters in those days came without air-conditioning, a deficiency which would gain momentum in equatorial waters or when tied up – sometimes for days – in the steamy heat of some tropical or subtropical port. Neither did cargo ships enjoy the comfort of stabilisers, which during the typhoon season would often make for a rough passage through the Indian Ocean or South China Sea.

Then again, nearer to home, the notoriously fickle waters of the Bay of Biscay seldom made for a calm passage. The thought of having to weather rough seas on a small boat might thus have persuaded many a landlubber or the less robust traveller to book a more stable passage on one of the P & O liners.

The privilege of travelling by freighter regretfully ended when container ships began to cross the oceans with substantially larger cargoes. Today, these giants will take the odd passenger on board, often providing four-star hotel accommodation and more importantly, stabilisers and air-conditioning. But will these vessels, not to mention the cruise ships catering for several thousand passengers, hold the same fascination? Will they imbue the traveller with the same spirit of adventure as a mid-twentieth-century cargo boat?

What then was the magic of seafaring on a 'banana boat'? Well, apart from port-hopping and seeing the world on affordable terms, passengers of a romantic, free-spirited disposition might explain that on a small merchant ship one never felt alone; that under clear skies and on unruffled waters, with no more than the muted drone of the ship's engine for background sound, one can hear the waves lapping against the hull; and that without the entertainment-oriented distractions of a large passenger ship one's mind is able to freewheel. And then, they might add, there are those tranquil nights in southern latitudes where the stars are more luminous and seemingly within reach of one's arm...

PART I

THE OUTWARD PASSAGE

Gibraltar – Hospital on the Rock

In June 1961 my husband, a Ministry of Defence Intelligence Officer serving with the British Security Forces in Berlin, received his posting to Hong Kong. As our three children – John, Andrew and Donald – were under the age of four, Army travel clerks advised us against the 26-hour flight to the Crown Colony – the time it took an Army-chartered Britannia aircraft in those days to cover the route. Surely, they said, such a long flight with only two refuelling stops would be hard on children of that age. Diplomacy did not allow them to point out the extra onus it would place on cabin staff and the difficulties of preparing special baby and bottle feeds when in flight, let alone the hopeless task of keeping toddlers content in their seats for eight to nine hours at a stretch. 'Go by sea,' they said, and so a passage was booked for us on a cargo vessel trading between London and Hong Kong by way of the Suez Canal, calling at Port Said, Aden, Port Swettenham (now known as Port Klang), Penang and Singapore.

We boarded the 8,500-ton Blue Line *Glenroy* in June. The ship looked exactly as I had imagined an older commercial vessel to look like: its hull was crying out for a fresh coat of paint, as did the railings and anything else that on a cruise ship would blind with its pristine whiteness. Derricks were swinging noisily forwards and backwards, depositing crates and hessian-wrapped bales into the two holds. I was seized by a spirit of adventure. For this was our chance to sail towards new horizons and set foot in foreign places which we could otherwise not afford to visit. Already my insatiably romantic mind was pondering the delights of being at sea in the Southern Hemisphere, and I ached to experience that

John and Andrew playing on deck

The *Glenroy*: Andrew and John at their cabin window

sense of freedom which allegedly had held famous sea travellers in thrall. My anticipation of life in Hong Kong whipped up images of chopsticks, rickshaws, opium dens and sleazy red-lantern bars of Suzi Wong fame; of old women wobbling on the stumps left by tightly bound feet, and of a colony said to have the most beautiful harbour views in the world.

I had provided well for the expected five weeks at sea. A large metal trunk contained an ample supply of Heinz baby food, milk powder, bottles and biscuits, as well as baby cream, suntan lotions and the first cellulose nappies. I had packed preparations for colic, diarrhoea, constipation, prickly heat and cuts, and did not forget such helpful items as a pushchair parasol, plasters, a thermometer and a plastic potty. Both as a mother and a qualified nurse I was leaving nothing to chance. For the older children there were Lego bricks, picture books, miniature toy cars and a shopful of colouring books and pencils.

The *Glenroy* had accommodation for twelve passengers and – what a comforting thought! – carried a ship's doctor. Our two cabins came with bunk beds and token facilities. My cabin, which I shared with John, our eldest, and the baby, also had a cot. The fact that it was anchored to the cabin wall by hooks and rope should have given me food for thought. As it was, any notion that could have spoilt my happy anticipation of the voyage ahead was far from my mind. Neither did the absence of air conditioning and stabilisers worry me at the time. I had never heard of either, anyway, and my memory of crossing the English Channel in 1948 in stormy weather on a small freighter and former troop carrier had long since dulled with time.

A flock of seagulls accompanied us out of the Thames Estuary, swooping low over the ship and under a sky which grew increasingly murky as we sailed along the Channel. A north-westerly wind soon began to roughen up the water and, as soon as we entered the Atlantic, squalls slapped the sea into sheets of white-crested waves. Immediately, my stomach began to protest against the pitching and tossing, forcing me to retire to my bunk. Perhaps not unreasonably

5

I began to doubt the wisdom of travelling to our new posting by sea ... and we were not even in the Indian Ocean yet! I wailed silently as I stared towards the cabin window, watching as it was pummelled and blinded by sea spray. The children, by contrast, remained blissfully unaffected, happy enough to make their way through their arsenal of toys.

Once we had passed the Straits of Gibraltar and sailed full steam into the Mediterranean, life on board picked up again. We lazily commuted between deckchairs, bar and dining room, while doing our best to look after one baby and two toddlers in the confined space of the ship.

It happened when we were halfway between Gibraltar and Malta: I was watching the distant coastline and my husband was lounging in a deckchair, immersed in an animated conversation with the first officer about the decimation of Britain's colonies, when a child's scream made us sit up in alarm. Bent on exploring, John, the three-year-old, had managed to wander off to a steep stairway, the gate of which a member of the crew had carelessly left open. Somehow the toddler must have slipped and toppled down. I raced to the scene, fearing the worst. But luckily, apart from some minor grazes where skin had come into contact with the sharp-edged metal treads, and a painful wrist, he did not appear any worse for his misadventure. The hastily summoned doctor cursorily examined the child and prescribed rest. I noticed that the good doctor was not too stable on his feet and that, although it was still early in the afternoon, his breath was heavily laced with alcohol.

An hour later John complained of a severe headache. He felt feverish and the thermometer registered a dramatic rise in body temperature. I requested another visit from the doctor. This time, however, his eyebrows shot up and he looked mystified.

'I'm afraid,' he began, 'your son may have injured his head. The symptoms suggest a slight fracture, perhaps a blood clot... It may affect the temperature-regulating centre in the brain... The child ought to be seen by a specialist. I'll have a word with the

Captain.' No smile. No reassurance. The worst scenario was developing in my mind.

The Captain did not cushion his words either and came straight to the point.

'I have contacted my shipping line, and they have given me permission to turn the ship around and sail back to Gibraltar. The British military hospital there has better diagnostic facilities than Malta. If your son has sustained a more serious injury he could be flown immediately back to a London hospital.'

As with the snap of a finger all my romantic aspirations for our time on board went backstage. Pangs of panic assailed me. After all, I had once swotted over anatomy and had worked in an operating theatre, so I knew the hazards of surgery. Thus the nightmare continued for the rest of the day, made even more real by my having to pack our suitcases again in case we would have to leave the ship.

It was dark when the ship dropped anchor offshore, in line with international health regulations that come into force whenever a vessel has a patient with an undiagnosed or suspect illness on board. A British harbour doctor was presently ferried to the ship and examined John for signs of meningitis or some other infectious disease. He was very professional, leaving us to clutch not at straws of hope but solid batons. 'Mind you,' he said when he saw my anxious face, 'I don't think there's anything seriously wrong with your son. We'll have him taken ashore and seen at the Army & Navy Hospital on the Rock.'

But now the Captain dampened my sense of relief.

'My shipping line allows me to wait for two hours,' he told my husband. 'If your wife and son aren't back by then I'm afraid you and the rest of the family will have to leave the ship. You must understand, we will have lost a whole day at sea.'

He looked uncomfortable, as if he were computing how much the delay would cost the company in pounds sterling.

Passengers and crew watched on as I climbed down a steep ladder into a motor launch and the child, wrapped in a blanket, was lifted down by a member of the crew. The moon was shedding a silvery light across the harbour and the distant Rock, and as the launch sped towards the pier the *Glenroy* assumed a spectral shade reminiscent of the *Flying Dutchman*'s phantom ship.

The child in my arms: 'Where are we going, Mummy?'

An ambulance was waiting, and soon its siren blasted its way through the narrow streets to the historic World War II military hospital. In one of its catacomb-like tunnels a surgical consultant, a medical specialist, a radiographer and senior lab technician were waiting for us in dinner jackets, having been called away from a party. A nurse took the child from me and I was told to wait.

Time passes slowly when terror is wrenching your guts. What if...? I was shivering in the alien chill of the tunnel, nervously checking my watch and staring at the door behind which my son's fate was being decided.

With half an hour to spare before the deadline ran out, the medical team emerged and returned him to my arms.

'You may take your son back to the ship,' said the internist. 'I phoned the Captain.' A broad smile ran over his face. 'The child's got glandular fever... Must have contracted it before you boarded the ship.' He handed me some tablets. 'This is an antibiotic, Aureomycin; it'll bring down the temperature.' And pointing to John's arm, which was now encased in plaster from cuff to elbow, he added: 'The boy has a greenstick fracture of the wrist. Nothing serious; it'll heal soon.'

Handshakes, good wishes. I heaved a monumental sigh of relief and stammered my thanks. My smile lit up the tunnel. My little world was back in its orbit.

Although by now it was well past midnight when we returned, a few passengers had stayed up on deck, watching developments a drink in hand, and now they expressed their delight at the happy outcome of what so easily could have ended in tragedy. The good doctor was nowhere to be seen. I returned John, now suitably medicated, to his bunk and unpacked our suitcases again. Yet sleep that night was slow in coming, as my mind kept reeling with the

Father with Andrew and Donald

events of the past twenty-four hours. Surely, I thought, our passage would now be all plain sailing. I finally fell asleep when the first rays of light seeped through the cabin window. For the moment it was left to the imagination how the ship's doctor's inability to diagnose a simple case of glandular fever and a broken wrist would affect his career and, more immediately, his position on board. Indeed, in the weeks to come, he would keep a noticeably low profile and even avoid 'happy hour' at the bar. However, medical duty required him to check up on the boy's progress. During such visits his bearing would demonstrate hostility towards the parents whose son's accident and illness had exposed his diagnostic blunder, if not professional inadequacy. (We later learned that the shipping company had sacked him.)

Under a blue and cloudless Mediterranean sky temperatures soon began to reach the nineties. John's condition had markedly improved, and now I could settle the patient in the pushchair in a shady part of the deck next to his siblings. His father would keep a proud eye on his progeny, whilst trying at the same time to gather the latest news from a three-day-old copy of the *Telegraph*. In between dozing and reading, I might assist baby Donald in his attempts to raise himself to an upright position, or make congratulatory noises whenever Andrew built another futuristic Lego structure with the apparent knowhow of a construction engineer. Mostly, however, time was running in the slow lane again.

The Suez Canal

While the *Glenroy* was waiting to be piloted into the harbour of Port Said, a flotilla of dhows and small boats raced towards the ship. Passengers were told to lock their cabin doors and windows, before an army of wild-looking Arabs was allowed to invade the gangways with their merchandise. Since the Egyptian authorities did not permit passengers to go ashore, the main deck soon became the stage for some passionate bargaining. Among the passengers, an elderly lady on her second round-trip to Hong Kong, handled the lengthy proceedings over the price of some table linen with the ease and shrewdness of one who has lived in Arab countries for many years. So did the retired Scottish colonel who seemed equally at home in the art of arriving at a mutually agreeable price. 'Foreigners,' he explained, 'who ignored the ritual of bargaining, or undertook it flippantly, earned nothing but contempt from the vendor.'

Two hours later the ship berthed and was loaded with tons of onions and potatoes for Hong Kong. There followed another wait until seven ships had assembled, enough to form a convoy and, safely distanced from each other, to be piloted into the Suez Canal, which President Nasser had nationalised in 1957.

I felt as excited at the vistas opening up as I had been when, as a five-year-old, I had first set eyes on the open sea at a Baltic resort. Here, though, on the Sinai Peninsular, a hazy range of hills rose naked from the desert, while on the western shore there opened up a boundless ocean of yellow-grey sand – the same desert panorama which, despite its biblical and nomadic history, Evelyn Waugh had once called 'the dullest in the world'.

11

The Suez Canal

We were halfway into the Canal when the convoy stopped and our vessel dropped anchor. A crew member informed passengers that owing to acute congestion in the Gulf of Suez we might be in for a long wait. Immediately the heat closed in on us. With not a breeze to sway a blade of grass, the gangway sizzled, and the air vibrated over the water which had the smoothness of velvet cloth. The stillness on board resembled that of a Spanish village at siesta time.

The sun was dipping towards the horizon like a huge blood orange when a chance to swim offered itself. A ladder was lowered and a member of the crew posted as a lifeguard. Yet, apart from a few deckhands, I was the only passenger to slip into the lukewarm water over which, in spectacular fashion, the setting sun was casting its final blush. Somehow, the experience seemed unreal, very personal and unforgettable.

I swam with languid strokes, looking towards the western bank where a slow-moving caravan now came into view, silhouetted against the picture-book sunset. It reminded me of travel stories I had read about the Arabian desert: of fearless, single-minded explorers and Victorian travellers who had braved hardships, ever-present thirst and long marches through arid wastes under a blistering sun. I thought of how they had pitched their tents at night, drank tea with Bedouins or slept next to their camels under a planetarium-domed sky, enfolded in an all-pervading silence which might be broken, now and then, by the bark of a camel...

Later that night – we were moving again, yet still at a paltry knot or two – the bar steward demonstrated how he could tell when the temperature exceeded 100°F. He placed a candle on a saucer and lit it. Before we could count to ten the candle bent over, doubled on itself and went out in a bath of wax. There came applause; the drinkers wiped the sweat off their faces and ordered another round. It would remain open to speculation whether such a display was standard seasonal entertainment in the Canal, in order to boost the ship's income from the bar, or whether it was intended to top up the steward's own purse by way of extra tips.

As the oppressive heat in the cabins promised to boycott sleep, we bedded ourselves on deck like campers. Here at least, a zephyr-like movement of air – generated by the ship's guarded speed – made for some light slumber. Once we reached the Red Sea, the waterway widened and the faster-moving ship created a welcome current of air which acted like a mental and physical tonic. The relief was, however, short-lived, for when we sailed into the Gulf of Suez the ship had to wait for hours, before being piloted into the Port of Aden. We were back in the cauldron of heat.

I knew nothing about our first port of call, except that it lay on a peninsula at the mouth of the Red Sea, and was a convenient harbour at the gateway to the Indian Ocean. Guessing that most passengers thought of Aden as just another hellishly hot, uncivilised place on the map, the Captain gave us a brief run-down on the Yemeni capital.

'Aden has been a strategic British Protectorate since 1935,' he said. 'In the fifties it saw many modern housing and mercantile developments, and its harbour is now one of the busiest in the world due to its oil bunkerage and ship-refuelling facility. Mind you, although they have cranes now, the dockers still work to their own time-clock. *Inshallah!* Also, in the Old Quarter, little has changed. It still paints a picture of nineteenth-century village life, except that the locals now wear flip-flops and many have a radio.'

Direction were given how to reach the NAAFI shop. What better amenity, I thought, to mark British military presence in some foreign outback.

Aden

We berthed at noon, at a time of day when supposedly 'wild dogs and Englishmen...' Well, we went ashore anyway. After all, we had some serious shopping to do. And since by now John's illness seemed to have run its course and his temperature was normal again, we decided to take him along.

A scorching wind was blowing from the Saudi Arabian desert, whirling up fine grains of sand. The glare of the sun and the whiteness of the flat-roofed houses created a blinding ambience of light. My husband was carrying baby Donald; I was pushing the buggy, in which our convalescent toddler had pride of place, while Andrew, fearful of all that foreignness around us, nervously clutched a fold of my dress.

Right away I felt as if we were on stage. Looking conspicuously Western, if not English, at a time when global tourism was still in its infancy, the sight of three small, fair-haired children and a pushchair with a parasol visibly intrigued the locals. They smiled at the children, passing what sounded like florid remarks on the blessing of having three sons. However, when they looked at their parents, the 'non-believers', and most pointedly at the mother who wore a dress that left her arms, shoulders and legs uncovered, their eyes darkened with hostility and cries of *Allah* went up, possibly in indignation of such an unholy sight.

Having just felt deliciously 'abroad', then increasingly alarmed at being unable to take our bearings in the foreign maelstrom, we found our way to the cocoon-like NAAFI compound and welcome British shopping outpost as if by radar. Here, suddenly feeling comfortably at home, we bought an inflatable paddling pool, plastic buckets, a child's watering can, packets of Kellogg's cornflakes and, with weeks on board still ahead, a collapsible playpen. Loaded with our purchases, and with our spirits soon clogged up by the heat and dust, we decided to take a short cut back to the harbour through a network of narrow lanes.

It proved to have been an unwise choice. Assaulted by a mixed bouquet of sewage, putrefaction and highly spiced cooking smells, we were followed by a bunch of fearsome-looking characters, who insisted we buy a 'genuine' Swiss watch, a German camera, carved wooden images of African deities, a back scratcher with an ivory handle, painted earthenware jugs and whatever other wares they were peddling. Scarecrows of beggars intimidated us by sidling up so close that we could smell the foul breath of rotting teeth; talon-like fingers moved menacingly in front of my husband's face. Cries accompanied us, '*Sahib, Sahib, baksheesh.*' A novice to such pestering, my husband was forced to carry the heavy playpen with one hand, while guarding the contents of his trouser pocket with

'MacKinnon's Veranda'

16

the other. In the pushchair, John now cradled his youngest brother, while I tried to cope with the rest of the shopping and the transport of two children in what in those days was no more than a flimsy folding-chair. The timely intervention of a policeman finally saved us from more harassment, or worse. Heaving under our acquisitions, we finally made it back to the ship.

Room for the paddling pool was found in a quiet and shady corner at the stern end of the deck, and a member of the crew hosed in sea water. The children were delighted, and in the days to come they would splash about, showering each other or watering the surrounding deck planks as if they were flower beds. It came as no surprise that our designated deck space, with its pool, playpen, pushchair, towels, deckchairs, a consortium of toys and other lounging gear, soon became known as 'MacKinnon's Veranda'.

Now that they had settled down on the ship, the children proved to be a never-ending source of amusement. Given a cloth, John would polish everything in sight on deck. Once, seen rubbing some specs from the foghorn, he explained he was cleaning where the 'tut-tut' was coming out. One evening, I caught him using my lipstick and blusher in an attempt to copy the make-up of his picture-book clown. Needless to say, the sight of his crimson, absurdly outlined lips and the flaming blotches on his cheeks, if not his beguiling smile of innocence, obviated any reprimand.

Andrew, too, provided his own brand of entertainment. Forever given to experimenting with independence, and full of a toddler's mischief, he often had bystanders in peals of laughter.

Donald, on the other hand, infected everyone around him with his beatific smile, and he never lacked for an audience whenever he tried to stand up, determined to leave the nest of his perambulator. I was, however, not amused when one day in the empty dining room he employed the legs of a chair for such exercise, during which the solid content of his nappy fell out on to the carpet. This mishap was followed by feverish activity on my part, trying to remove the offensive evidence before a steward or passengers arrived on the scene. Inwardly, however, I could not help chuckling at the guilty party who, by now a little *Homo erectus*, was making jubilant noises and looked like a climber who had just reached a Himalayan peak.

Years later he would aspire to much greater heights.

A Tempest

As soon as we had left the Gulf of Aden, we sailed through a belt of exquisite calm. The sea wore a silver shine and the timid swell of the water no more than caressed the hulls. However, the peaceful scene was not to last. Twenty-four hours later, and by now in the Indian Ocean, low banks of clouds were building up. As in a sudden change of mood, the surface of the sea turned dark and troubled, and it was not long before a squally wind whipped up waves which slapped against the hull, at first teasingly, but soon gaining bullying force. Members of the crew dashed around, fixing ropes to the corridors and checking the anchorage of the cot in my cabin. 'Routine measures,' they said, 'whenever a typhoon is ready to strike.'

By nightfall the ship was feeling the full force of the storm, yielding to every gust and swell, rolling and pitching, then bucking again like a rodeo bull. In tandem with the battering winds, the sea now rose in broad, white-plumed sheets which thumped against the hull, drowning out even the sound of the ship's engine. When, finally, rain belted down, our vessel seemed awesomely vulnerable, a mere speck in the ocean. Bunk-bound, we bravely tried to ride out the brunt of the storm, envying our youngest who was strangely unaffected by the turmoil outside and still demanded his bedtime bottle. Yet, never had such a task required more skill of me. Swaying in all directions, as dictated by the movements of the vessel, I tried not to scald myself with hot water from the Thermos flask, nor to spill half its contents when filtering it through the narrow neck of the bottle. I felt giddy from the heavings of my stomach, and now and then I was flung from one side of the cabin to the other, clinging on to bottle and flask as if they were holy relics. Lovingly I eyed my bed. But maternal duty allowed no such self-indulgence, particularly when the subject of my love and care was bouncing up and down in his cot in anticipation.

Having attended to the moans and groans of the rest of the family, I finally sought comfort in a horizontal position. However, any repose I may have found there was short-lived. During a particularly strong lurch of the ship the cabin door opened. Hadn't I closed it properly? Could the violent movement of the vessel have unlatched a weak lock? Whatever the cause, it would not have mattered an iota had not, at that very moment, the four-year-old daughter of fellow passengers appeared at the open door in her nightdress, holding on to its frame with one hand, and had not, with the next roll of the battered ship, the door swung heavily home, catching the little girl's finger and all but dismembering it. Her piercing cries brought her parents to the scene, who shouted abuse both at me and my husband, whom I had hastily summoned.

We never found out who or what had been responsible for the accident. But rather than blaming themselves for letting their child wander along the ship's corridor in the middle of a storm, and being deaf to my attestations of innocence, the parents lost no time in declaring us responsible for the misadventure. And they made it quite clear that they would sue us for negligence as soon as we reached Singapore. Whereupon they sought the ship doctor's own particular brand of medical attention.

For the rest of the passage to Singapore, and while the girl's finger was healing, they refused to speak to us, while we tried to avoid them, at least as far as this was possible in the confined space of the ship. (After the family disembarked at Singapore we never heard from them again, nor did we receive a legal summons. Under the circumstances, any case against us would surely have been dismissed by a court of law and negligence rather laid at the parents' own door.)

Rough seas continued during the night and for most of the following day. The steward was kept busy serving tea and water biscuits to cabin-bound passengers and volunteering advice on how best to cope with prolonged seasickness. He divulged that at least one passenger was still enjoying life on board: the retired Colonel, a man of parade-ground posture, sharp-cut features and a drill-sergeant's voice, who had earlier laughed off the 'inconvenience' of a storm. Having seen many years of service in India, he claimed to have grown his sea legs during frequent passages to and from the Subcontinent. To the distress of those who had fallen victim to the rage of the sea, he had allegedly made short shrift of an English breakfast and a *rijsttafel* (an Indonesian meal of eggs, meat, fish and fruit, mixed with rice and served in separate dishes) at lunch, as well as a good many drams of whisky, which he praised for its stomach-calming property. The only concession he was said to have made to the elements was to leave his pipe unlit.

Once the wind had lulled and the sun was forcing her way through the straggling clouds, passengers gingerly repaired to the deck and into the dining room, their pasty faces contrasting sharply with the Colonel's ruddy complexion and healthy appetite, both of which were the envy of the convalescents. Asked about his formula to ward off the onslaught of *mal de mer*, he gave credit to his constitution and to an old soldier's fondness of the golden tipple.

Thus normality returned on board. The men wore shorts and open-neck shirts; the ladies sleeveless dresses or modest beachwear. The bar steward served gallons of long and not-so-long drinks, and dinner became once again the highlight of the day. I, too, was back in a holiday mood, determined to enjoy a *dolce far niente*, and looking forward to going ashore at our next port of call.

Port Swettenham

The ship dropped anchor offshore late in the morning. Not a breeze stirred over the Malaysian port, known in those years for its ramshackle wharf, rusting sheds and warehouses, and unpopular with cargo vessels because of the slow and chaotic handling of freight. True enough, we had to wait twenty-four hours offshore before being allowed to berth.

Soon the hatches opened and derricks swung into action. A gang of swarthy, vociferous dock workers came on board, naked to the waist and sporting pieces of cloth around their heads like pirates. They began to offload and load cargo at their own pace, unhurriedly, now and then resting on their haunches or unrolling their straw mats to go to sleep in some corner of the ship. Meanwhile, passengers fled from the noisy activity on board and their stifling cabins. Most of them followed the Captain's advice and made straight for the Seamen's Club. 'It has a swimming pool and ice-cold drinks,' he said. 'Just follow the signs.'

Although any ambitious sightseeing was bound to be short-lived in the steaming heat, we decided first to have a look around, before seeking some transport to take us to the city of Kuala Lumpur and its famous mosques and pagodas. We briefly paused at the market, a hotchpotch of local women, free-roaming children, screeching slaughter-bound chickens, mongrel dogs and scurrying rats. An overpowering bouquet of fish, spices, sewage and rotting, flyblown meat, which hung like miasma over the site, put haste into our steps.

We set off on foot down the main and only road to the Malayan capital. The road was nothing more than sun-baked soil. It was lined with hibiscus trees in their crimson glory, and by coconut and banana trees whose foliage provided us with a modicum of shade. Behind them, often encroached upon by shoulder-high ferns, thatched huts on stilts and tumbledown sheds backed onto liana-webbed dense jungle. Once we had passed the last outpost of local civilisation, without sighting a single car, I became conscious of a hothouse silence fitfully broken by muted sounds from within the undergrowth and the dome of the jungle. By now the sun stood in its zenith. Donald had fallen asleep in his pushchair, and his brothers had to be pulled along as if they had lead under their feet. My own legs were labouring, too, while my inner eye projected images of iced lemon tea and the haven of a swimming pool.

Just then a car materialised. Although looking like a candidate for the scrapyard, the cruising vehicle proclaimed in bold-lettered English that it was a taxi for hire, ferrying passengers to and from the capital. My husband, now visibly thirsting for a cold beer rather than for the sight of golden minarets, and perhaps dreading the long trot back to the port on foot, hailed the driver. 'Can you take us to Kuala Lumpur?' he asked, without even negotiating the fare.

Squeezed into the veteran conveyance like proverbial sardines, we bravely held out for the best of five miles before Donald started to cry and his brothers to whine with thirst. Their father, a large handkerchief in constant sweat-dabbing action, and his breathing audibly troubled by the steambath ambience, gasped at the driver, 'Take us back to Port Swettenham, to the Seamen's Club.' Alas, never again would we have a chance to visit the city's famous landmarks.

We soon met up with our fellow passengers, all of whom had resisted the urge to explore local colour or venture inland. Here now was heaven. Cool drinks. A bite to eat. A welcoming pool. Our relief was infinite. For the remainder of our shore outing the children splashed happily in the pool, in which the adults, half-submerged, a drink within easy reach, discussed world affairs in general and life in local climes in particular.

When time dictated our return to the ship, and we wound our

way back along a narrow path, life in the jungle was erupting again. The heat was bearable now. Colours had intensified, exotic butterflies were flitting about, and from the crowns of trees the avian population delivered orchestral sounds.

Back on board, the last hold was being closed, derricks grew silent and the rumbustious troupe of dock hands went ashore. Passengers slumped into wicker chairs, summoned the bar steward and welcomed the light sea breeze much like Inuits might greet the re-emergence of the sun.

That night, on our way to Penang, I bedded down on deck next to baby Donald, who was fast asleep in his pushchair. A full moon hung in the sky like an outsize silver balloon, cutting a glade of light over the sea, while the stars in their constellations, and brilliance, not seen in our Northern Hemisphere, created the effect of a magical planetarium.

The sight held me in thrall. For a few moments I was a child again, a dreamer, a romantic and, on my solitary island of meditation, a lone human being confronting the infinity of space, and what twenty years later Malcolm Muggeridge in *A Spiritual Journey* would call 'The Cloud of Unknowing'. Well, it was just that kind of night, that kind of sky, to which the steady rumble of the ship's engine and the soft swell of the sea formed a cathedral-like background.

Penang

We arrived in Penang in the early hours of the morning. As loading was expected to take most of the day, passengers were given ample shore leave. It was already very hot, but a south-westerly breeze made the heat and humidity feel less oppressive. A launch took us ashore. Duly equipped with nappies, suncream, bottled drinks, pushchair and camera, we hired a taxi for the day and asked the driver to take us around the major sites.

We first stopped at the foot of the Snake Temple, whose well-trodden, seemingly never-ending steps were more than likely to

Penang Hill

27

Temple

prompt Buddhist worshippers to repent their sins. Like visitors to a zoo, we stared at the cobras which lay curled up or were writhing on the temple's effigies and altars. While for me this was a mesmerising, though subliminally menacing sight, for the children live snakes were a novelty they would have liked to touch like domestic pets. Needless to say, we soon escaped this disquieting tableau.

More alien sights would open up as the taxi needled its way through the Chinese quarters, whose colourful and teeming street life gave us a foretaste of Hong Kong. Having safely manoeuvred through this claustrophobic area, our driver proceeded to Penang Hill, where we admired a breathtaking panorama before climbing more steps to a pagoda-topped temple and monastery. Sauntering around with the curiosity of European visitors, I took in all the manifestations of an alien religion as a child might today study dinosaurs or science-fiction characters. As a Christian, for whom Eastern religions and cultures were sadly still a closed book, I was taken aback by it all: the oversized, voluptuous busts of Buddha and other deities; their gilded, garish-coloured opulence, the lavish offerings of fresh food and the intoxicating scent of a myriad of burning joss-sticks. Somehow, I could not help comparing the icon of a pot-bellied crimson-cheeked Buddha with the poignant Christian image of Jesus on the Cross, or with the Virgin Mary holding the Christ Child in her arms. My comfortable Western concept of how the dead were left to lie in a dignified state while awaiting burial or cremation shrank back from the sight of small square boxes stacked in a courtyard, each of which allegedly contained a body crammed into a diminutive state like a parcelled commodity prior to disposal by fire.

Strangely enough, it was at this point that I suddenly realised how little I knew about foreign cultures, and how much I still had to learn; that since the end of the war the erratic course of my life, and my happy years of motherhood, had often by necessity curbed or held back any intellectual challenges and ambitions. What I knew about art, music and English literature I had learnt before

Penang Beach

29

my marriage; what I still remembered of history, geography and German literature I had learnt at school. Now, as if being allowed a glimpse into the future, I knew that this accidental and as yet dull awakening would steadily grow into a lust for study and knowledge, into a pursuit that would continue to enrich and enliven me well into my dotage.

Sated for the moment with Buddhist culture, we were ready to spend the rest of the day at Penang beach. A short ride past Malayan villages, a spice plantation and coconut grove took us to a palm-fringed beach – a paradisical stretch of white pristine sand blessedly still devoid of package holiday-makers and all the trappings of mass tourism.

Although the sea was calm and gentle breakers touched the shore like afterthoughts, our driver – who would presently retire under palms for his siesta – warned us not to let the toddlers walk even into the first shallow feet of water, as the seabed reclined sharply to a depth where even adults' feet no longer touched the bottom. Yet the waves that rolled upon the beach still allowed the youngsters to splash about and build a sandcastle. For the rest of the afternoon heaven was sun, sea and sand.

A delicious silence prevailed, somehow not violated, but rather sharpened by the sounds of the sea. The toddlers were sieving sand, digging water troughs and sculpting a moated castle, while little Donald probed the texture of the fine sand, throwing the odd handful towards the work in progress, not wanting to be excluded from his brothers' masterly construction.

Happiness in a nutshell. Happiness that comes, cameo-like, capturing, savouring the quality of the hour. And now memories rose, treading softly, neither accusing nor questioning, nor intruding upon the present idyll. I thought of my own parents who, during three of my August school holidays, had dispatched me, their only child, from the age of seven to children's holiday homes for the length of their own travels.

One such 'home' had bordered the Friesian North Sea coast where, even in August, the chilly water temperature did not invite bathers and the wind was always fresh and squally. Another home had been on the Baltic coast, where the sea was warm enough for swimming, and where at low tide the beach would be covered with pieces of pure amber. It was here that I had caught chickenpox, which confined me for weeks to an isolation cubicle in the sickbay. My earliest holiday 'evacuation' was to a place in what were then Germany's Silesian mountains, the Riesengebirge, where the air was bracing and cows scuttled over the meadows with bells around their necks. I recall that discipline was strict, especially where fickle eaters were concerned. Numerous were the lunches when spinach or a watery chocolate pudding were on the menu; when I sat staring into the dark, turd-like mess, unable to swallow a single mouthful, and was punished in return by having to go without *Adendbrot*, my evening meal.

How fortunate our children were, I thought. I was sure we would never put them through the heartbreak of seasonal rejection, so that their parents could go to Venice or enjoy the elegant ambience of a German spa. Our children would not be subjected to weeks of separation, sweetened by their parents' promise of seaside fun or exhilarating walks in the country of *Rübezahl*, the friendly spirit of the mountains.

Donald's cry for help ended my reflections. A grain of sand had found its way into one of his eyes and he wanted 'Mummy' to remove it. It was also time for me to admire the finished castle, praise to which Father's sonorous voice lent hearty support.

We stayed on this golden beach until the sun began to dip towards the horizon. Our driver took us back to the ship's berth and, rewarded with a handsome tip, beamed a broad smile at the English family. Soon the ship's engine splattered back to life and the vessel eased herself out of the harbour and into the Straits of Malacca.

Singapore

Singapore Harbour 1961

A short taxi ride took us through the docks and past the main sights, before dropping us at a market in the older part of the city. Just a quick whiff of something that couldn't be found in front of elegant government buildings or at the front of statues, we thought; a look at something non-sanitized – life around the alleys of Singapore.

The lively, colourful scene of a large oriental street market would later become a familiar sight, but it was one which would never cease to fascinate me. Stalls selling dried fish, live snakes and chickens; fly-weary meat, exotic fruit and vegetables rubbed shoulders with songbirds in cages, fortune-tellers, letter-writers, mongrels in pens, Chinese noodle-kitchens, and hawkers of herbal medicines, potency-enhancing powders and whatever else might provide happiness or flatter vanity.

It took some effort to wheel the pushchair through the throng of shoppers, and we were not amused when their hands tried to

Singapore Botanical Gardens

touch the children's hair, as if physical contact with their blond locks would bring good fortune. At one point, having got stuck in the mêlée, we found ourselves surrounded by people who, impenetrable smiles on their faces, stared at us as if we were freaks of nature. Perhaps they applauded our audacity as 'white devils' to walk in their midst. Beaming our best smiles back, we threaded our way out and hired another taxi to take us to the city's Botanical Gardens.

Here, the vast crowns of ancient trees afforded welcome shade. The air was heavy with the scent of exotic blooms, and birdsong replaced the cacophony of the streets. Once the sun had reached its zenith, a paradisical calm hovered over the gardens. Soporific though it was, we ambled along, visiting the famous orchid nurseries and feeding free-roaming monkeys, before making our way to the seafront NAAFI Club. With its Olympic-sized swimming pool, nappy-changing facilities, a children's playground and snack bar it was a godsend for a family with small children. We stayed until it was time to re-embark.

Ever since the ship had entered Malaysian waters, and especially during its passage through the narrow Strait of Malacca, the sea had been as calm as any landlubber could hope for. By now, the idle days on board and the galley's tasty Indonesian and Chinese dishes had become a way of life. During the day the children amused themselves in the paddling pool or devoted time to serious play. The adults would read, stare across the sea, doze or just contemplate life from their wicker chairs. The sun had bronzed our skin, the sea air sharpened our appetite. We would have been happy if time had stood still, trapping us as long as it took to tire of this sweet idleness.

It was now well over three weeks since we boarded the *Glenroy* at the London wharf. Another week or two of what we hoped would be plain sailing would take us to Hong Kong. However, plain sailing was not what the sea gods had in store for us. For as soon as we entered the South China Sea, a change of weather was afoot. The Captain himself delivered the news: 'I'm afraid we'll be running into another tropical storm. There is a chance that it will upgrade to a typhoon. It's the season for them in these parts.'

Reality was back in the saddle.

In what by now seemed to be routine procedure, we folded up the pool, deposited any loose items in our cabins and watched as the ship's safety regime swung into action. With the precarious preparation of Donald's bedtime drink during the last storm still fresh in my mind, I prepared his bottle well in advance. Then, huddling all together, we waited for hell to break loose.

Once the barometer had fallen sharply, an unnerving air of expectancy hung over the vessel, and it was not long before the angry colour of the sea announced the imminence of violent weather and the sea, steel grey by now, began to swell. When, finally, the wind had worked itself into a frenzy, reaching gale-force, and foam-crested waves were crashing upon deck, I felt a flutter of fear in my guts. To add to the pandemonium outside, the sky now opened and rain shot down like machine-gun fire. The combined elements were having a feast.

The feast was to last two days.

Once again, Donald was unaffected by the vile movements of the ship, while I and the rest of the family lay groaning and retching in our bunks. And we certainly found no consolation in the steward's news that the Colonel had only nibbled at his sweet and sour pork at dinner, before retiring early to his cabin, a bottle of whisky under his arm.

We finally arrived in Hong Kong on 28 July 1961, having been at sea for close to five weeks.

PART II

LIFE IN HONG KONG

No Welcome for the New Arrivals

Hong Kong Harbour

The sun stood high in an azure sky when the *Glenroy* entered Victoria Harbour and berthed at Kowloon pier. No brass band welcomed us, no crowds of onlookers to wave us into port. Instead, as soon as we walked down the gangway an oven-like heat clamped down on us. The spectacular view across the turquoise water made some amends: the constant flow of sampans, water 'taxis' and ferries, large ships lying at anchor and, over on Hong Kong Island, the cluster of high-rise buildings reaching like fingers into the sky, gleaming in the sunshine.

Hong Kong Harbour

For me, it was a momentous arrival. I was conscious of a pleasurable, if cautious, anticipation of the years ahead. Of exciting new experiences and challenges. Of a notebook lying open, waiting for a diarist.

A member of my husband's Ministry of Defence and British Forces Security Unit greeted us with the unwelcome news that owing to a hiccup – well, he admitted, crossed wires between the Army quartermaster and London – family accommodation would not be available for us for some months, and that we would have to live in a hotel until such a time as we found a flat to rent.

Star Ferry

'Mind you,' he added, 'flats of an acceptable standard and location are few and far between, and the rents are prohibitive. The housing shortage in Hong Kong...'

My husband reacted predictably. He uttered a medium-sized expletive and referred to the QM and his London counterpart as 'ineffective pen-pushers', whereupon we bundled into a car and had ourselves taken to a Kowloon hotel.

The thirty-bed Hotel Capitol, a cheap lodging house for commercial travellers, stood on Kowloon's busiest road and backed onto a brothel. It would not have rated a single star in Britain. However, even if our temporary hotel accommodation was to be subsidized by the MoD, the Capitol was all we could afford.

The large lino-floored room contained four single beds and a cot, a long table, a few chairs and an ancient air conditioner. The hostelry had no dining room and no lounge. Meals had to be ordered by room service. However, our taste buds rejected the Cantonese-adulterated version of what passed for 'English' dishes. The children, who normally ate whatever was on the table, would screw up their faces after the first mouthful. And so did their parents. In order to keep malnutrition at bay, I now bought European tinned food and had it heated up in the hotel kitchen for dinner,

41

View from Hong Kong Island to Kowloon and the mainland

while for lunch I would make sandwiches. Sometimes we would have a typical Chinese meal in a restaurant favoured by local families. This would lead to a lifelong love of Chinese cuisine.

The handling of food stuff in our room soon posed a problem, as the resident ants and cockroaches began to claim their share. They would troop across the floor and up the table like an invading army, devouring every cornflake, bread or biscuit crumb, and feasting on the spillage of soft drinks. As the days went by, I was sure that they had passed word to colonies on other floors that the halcyon days of feeding had arrived.

There was something else we had to face. Tap water in the Colony was now restricted to four hours a day, with the prospect of further cuts to come. In any case it was not potable and thus imposed further strain on families with small children, particularly since a recent outbreak of cholera, carried in from China through Macao, demanded strictest observation of hygiene and food preparation.

There was also the steady din of traffic and the labouring drone

Queen's Road, Hong Kong Island

of the veteran air conditioner, both of which did not aid restful sleep. The adults were worst affected, and it was not long before we raised our voices. This, in turn, led to petulant behaviour in the children who, normally delightfully content and self-absorbed in their play, would suddenly quarrel over every Lego brick or picture-book, while the youngest would cry at the slightest provocation.

'When are we going home, Mummy?' asked John one day. And I knew what he meant was the life of home-cooked meals and restful sleep, the garden where he could ride his tricycle and play ball. This was the place he knew as 'home'.

Gradually, the days turned into a manageable, if reluctant routine. While my husband was working at the BFSO offices at the nearby Whitfield Barracks, I went shopping with the children or looked around for a flat and a playground. The heat and high humidity, though, continued unrelenting, water remained a precious commodity, and life in our vermin-infested hotel room frequently tested even my mental and physical stamina.

43

Not surprisingly, the Hong Kong flu virus soon found easy victims in us. One by one we went down with a high temperature, sore throat and a nasty cough. To top it all, Donald started teething again, which required mother's loving attention. The Army doctor visited, swinging thermometer, stethoscope and spatulae into action. He called for bed rest and a high fluid intake, and wrote out five individual prescriptions. As often happens in similar circumstances, the onus fell on the mother, and despite my own soaring temperature and wobbly knees I went round cooling foreheads, dispensing drinks, administering cough medicines, and generally trying to keep the sickbay in a survival spirit.

Three weeks after our arrival the Army Labour Office sent us an amah (maidservant and/or nanny) to assist me in my maternal duties. Aho was a very likeable Hong Kong-born woman in her late thirties. The children and I took to her immediately, and she would soon prove to be a godsend. Soon afterwards we moved into a semi-furnished three-bedroom flat in College Road, North Kowloon. It was light and airy and had a ceiling fan in every room. However, while with our departure from the Capital Hotel we may have stepped up a rung on the local housing ladder, our new householder status came with a drawback: the extreme noise

Kai Tak Airport strip (1961)

44

Kowloon City: Aircraft on approch to Kai Tak

Aho

Swimming pool at USRC

pollution caused by large BOAC and Cathay Pacific aircraft coming in to land at, or taking off from, neighbouring Kai Tak Airport. We had moved right under their flight path! Even earplugs would not have dampened the aural assault when the planes passed over

Children in rickshaw

46

our top-floor flat so low that we could count the screws on their underbellies. And as if the close-up of propellered flying machines were not enough, we would many times a day, and often past midnight, experience seconds of a deafening roar, accompanied by a whistling which, subliminally, reminded the Berliner in me of the Allied carpet-bombing in 1944 and 1945. Then the prospect of death or mutilation had been ever-present, particularly when a bomb would stop whining overhead too early, as this indicated a direct hit just seconds or metres away. The sensation had become so ingrained in my subconscious that even now I would instinctively duck for the length of a breath.

The new flat, which had come with no more than a double bed and a large dining table, soon filled up with odd pieces of furniture which I bought at auctions or had cheaply made by backstreet cabinetmakers. The children had ample space to play, and our new amah was happy to move in with us, even if not too pleased with her mean-sized, basic en-suite accommodation. She would cook, clean, wash and deal with the ubiquitous kitchen cockroaches. She also grew fond of the children.

Membership of the United Services Recreation Club, which boasted two swimming pools, tennis courts and a pleasant shaded sitting area, finally added a little gloss to everyday life. More importantly, it offered temporary relief from the energy-sapping daytime heat. Taxis being cheap, I would now take the children for a swim every afternoon. Thus, in no time Donald learnt how to keep afloat, while his siblings swam and dived as if they had been born with a pool at the back of our former Berlin garden.

Three months later we were offered a first-floor three-bedroom flat in an Army officers' rented block in Perth Street or Ba Fu Gai. It came with spacious rooms, ceiling fans, a six-metre balcony and separate quarters for two amahs. Facing vacant, rising ground, and flanked by hibiscus shrubs, the street ran up to a small roundabout backed by park-like greenery, thus forming a traffic-shy cul-de-sac, a safe playing and cycling area for children.

Ba Fu Gai

Here our life assumed at last a pleasing degree of normality, a working formula for the kind of haven which allowed all of us before long to think of our temporary abode as 'home'.

Beasts and Beasties

Like every subtropical and tropical place on earth, Hong Kong had its own brand of bugs, vermin, insects and wildlife. Like everyone else we had to live with minor endemic infections known in the local vernacular as 'Hong Kong tummy', 'Hong Kong ear' and 'Hong Kong eye', which kept the Army family doctor busy. Vaccinations against cholera and typhus were mandatory, as the threat of an outbreak was ever-present at a time when hundreds of refugees from the Chinese mainland were flocking into the Colony every day. Special precautions had also to be taken in the preparation of food. Fruit and vegetables were washed in a light permanganate solution; water was boiled and bottled for drinking. However, none of us was immune to an occasional viral attack, to infections found in every other latitude from the Arctic to the Southern Archipelago. Otherwise, personal and kitchen hygiene, as well as a healthy immune system, proved to be the best prophylactic.

There were no guidelines as to how to handle local pests and predatory wildlife.

For me, *almost* topping the list of fearsome Hong Kong beasties was the cockroach, or *Blatta orientalis*. The colour of polished mahogany, the breed was omnivorous and largely nocturnal. They never hunted alone, but came in great scurrying armies. Squeezing through the narrowest of spaces, their sense of smell would soon locate every crumb of bread, every morsel of food carelessly left about. To see such a steel-plated brigade foraging in the kitchen was the stuff of which nightmares are made. They also seemed to have a cat's nine lives, for their shell-like armour did not crush

49

easily underfoot. To kill a beetle outright would involve the human hunter in a battle of wits and several murderous strikes.

An even greater horror, though, was the huge, winged cockroach, a descendant of the extinct reptile species *pterodactyl*, which was infinitely larger and more voracious than the common kitchen type. It would fly through an open window at night, seeking out whatever was its preference, including human blood and body fluids. If the window was shut, it would vexedly bounce against the pane with the thud of an imprisoned bumble bee, before looking for access elsewhere. Like most people I confess to having a natural aversion to big black beetles and giant spiders. Most of them are not a threat to humans, but no term is abusive enough for this giant flying cockroach which could win itself a starring role in a horror film.

One night two of these terrifying insects nearly caused me a heart attack. They came through the bedroom window, which – owing to the oppressive heat and ineffective cooling power of the fan – I had left open, curtains undrawn. I was brutally waken around midnight by a sharp pain. There, on my pillow, inches away from my face and in the path of a moonbeam, were two monsters feasting on the blood and serum oozing from a cut on my finger. Needless to say, in this spectral setting my heart was thumping away as if I had just completed a hundred-metre sprint. My shriek woke my husband who, not being amused at being roused from sleep, merely turned over, muttering indignation. It was thus left to me to take retaliatory action against the two loathsome gobblers. However, possibly used to the unfriendly behaviour of humans, they managed to evade my slipper and flew back out of the window. Still shaking, I thoroughly disinfected my finger, before hiding it under a plaster and, curtains now drawn, sweated out the rest of the night.

In another nocturnal horror story a rat took the leading role. Following heavy rainfall and local flooding, John, our five-year-old, prodded me awake. 'Mummy, there's something in the toilet,' he cried. On examination I found a large rat trying to scramble out. Male assistance was called for. My husband, cursing Hong Kong vermin and rats in particular, finally managed to push the offender back into the sewer. Next morning I gave my little rat-spotter a lecture on vermin. Trying not to destroy the toddler's *Wind in the Willows*-inspired image of 'Ratty', I explained that the hopeful invader had been an evil disease-carrying cousin of that friendly water vole and that at all cost it had to be kept away from homes and their surroundings. 'Has Moly got an evil cousin, too?' asked the keen reader of the children's classic. I replied in the negative, not wishing to elaborate on how moles were in fact the curse of gardeners who liked their lawns to be as smooth as

New Territories – 'jungle walk'

51

Author's husband feeding a monkey

putting greens. And while we were hot on the subject, I gathered the children around me and told them about man's uneasy relationship with beasts and beasties, and the loveable role some animals play in children's stories and picture books.

We did not have to go to the zoo to watch the canniness and alertness of monkeys. Just beyond the high-rise housing estates, where the occasional tiger was sometimes spotted in the jungle-like vegetation, they could be encountered swinging through the trees. They were also evident in rural markets, where they stole the produce and generally pestered the vendors; they even were known to bite a grown man. Walkers in the New Territories unfamiliar with such simian behaviour ran the risk of being taught a painful lesson.

We ourselves made our acquaintance with these long-tailed, pink-faced animals during a Sunday stroll. On a well-trodden path amid dense vegetation a female monkey blocked our way, eyeing us, her head tilted slightly, a hand outstretched in silent appeal like a beggar. My husband, fascinated by such a cute mock-human mannerism, offered her a piece of banana which she ungraciously accepted before running off. Suddenly, what I took to be a male, owing to its size and aggressive display of teeth, shot out of a tree and bit his apparent rival – my husband – in the leg. The nasty bite, which caused profuse bleeding, required urgent medical attention. For days my husband limped around with a dour face, though his sad story only won him ready laughs and very little sympathy. Needless to say, he never fed a wild monkey again, whatever its sex or winsome pose.

Hong Kong also provided a perfect habitat for various species of snakes. While now and then a housewife might find a cobra or adder lying curled up in her living room or kitchen, the removal of which would require special handlers, it was always advisable to tread carefully in Kowloon's jungle-like hinterland, in high grass, among clumps of bamboo or along one of the dried-up water courses in the New Territories.

Snakes, for some reason, also favoured the sporting ambience of the Royal Hong Kong golf course at Fanling. My husband once neatly hooked a three-foot viper out of the rough in which, seconds earlier, I had been searching for a stray ball. On another occasion, he was unable to hole his ball for par, because an ominous-looking serpent was lying curled up around the flagpole, ready to spit venom at any putter who dared to shift it. Not inclined to end up as a casualty, my husband abstained from moving the obstacle and accorded himself a par on his scorecard.

Apart from snakes, flying insects, rats and swarms of creepy-crawlies, the sickly looking dogs and cats which roamed the street markets and raided dustbins posed the all-too-real danger of rabies. It was, therefore, good policy not to get too close to such an animal, nor to try and stroke it. Yet, while one day I was strolling with the children through a Kowloon City market, and my attention was momentarily diverted by the sight of some revolting-looking food item, Andrew seized the opportunity to touch a scrawny mongrel which was tied by a short length of string to the leg of a stall. The animal, possibly more used to kicks than gentle patting,

United Services Recreation Club, Kowloon

bit the child's hand, snarled and bared its teeth like an enraged Rottweiler; only the mean length of the leash kept it from inflicting serious injury. Alarmed by the possible implications of the bleeding bite, I sought immediate medical attention. Right enough, without a minute to lose, the doctor reported the incident to the police, whose officers went out to locate the dog and had it tested for rabies. For days we anxiously waited for the result. Thankfully it proved negative.

Neither was the sea safe to swim in all the year around. Come October, people were advised not to swim in the waters off the islands because of the danger of sharks and the annual invasion of huge, poisonous jellyfish. Anyhow, even during the summer months, the waters around some of the popular beaches could prove a health hazard, as junks, passing or anchored close by, used to dump rubbish and ordure overboard, which an inshore wind or the incoming tide would then carry towards the beach and the swimmers, making especially children prone to eye and ear infections. But then, privileged as we were, we could always escape to unspoilt beaches by car and boat, or use the USRC's swimming pools and gardens – a haven for British families during the hot season. Life in Hong Kong would not have been half as enjoyable without this facility. Here, at an early age the children became competent swimmers.

Scares

Although we maintained an uneasy relationship with Hong Kong's 'beasties', we soon learnt to live with them. We were, however, not spared some other, more serious frights.

I was one day rushed to the military hospital on Hong Kong side with pain from a suspected ectopic pregnancy. While the tentative diagnosis pointed to the need for an immediate operation, the surgeon preferred to wait and have me closely monitored. Perhaps he was taking a gamble as a deterioration of my condition might well have had a fatal outcome. Yet, as it turned out, the good surgeon's waiting game paid off. Not by some miracle happening inside the reproductive organ in question, but by the approach of typhoon Wanda, which turned out to be one of the most destructive regional storms of the sixties.

While some weather changes, particularly those preceded by an abrupt drop in atmospheric pressure, are known to affect some people with arthritic joints or scar tissue, my own weather sensitivity – in this case an extreme response to an impending major storm – had mocked a serious gynaecological condition. Yet, oddly, even before HK radio had issued a severe weather warning, and while the first winds were still riding gently through the trees, my textbook symptoms disappeared and I was given a clean bill of health. By the time I was on my way home, the barometer had reached its nadir. Typhoon Wanda was about to strike.

To this day I wonder whether my case taught the surgeon something about morbid weather sensitivity, a subject which most likely is still not covered in medical school. Interestingly, my own body's reaction to the advent of freak weather or some electromagnetic changes in the atmosphere is still as acute today as it was in my younger days. No wonder, then, that my friends see in me an early weather forecaster, to be consulted whenever they plan an al fresco event.

In densely populated Hong Kong skin infections were endemic. Owing to their ease of contagion, and despite paying special attention to hygiene, they would frequently find easy victims in the children of Western families.

We had been two years in the Colony when Andrew contracted impetigo, a nasty skin affection which severely tested not only the four-year-old but also his 'barrier-nursing' mother. The Army family doctor, seemingly not familiar with the dermatological condition, prescribed some ointment (which was to prove totally ineffective) and assumed a time-will-heal attitude. The continued suffering of my little patient finally made me take drastic action. I went to see the nurse manager of the new British Hospital in Kowloon, who – as coincidences go – turned out to be the former ward sister under whom, ten years earlier, I had been working as a student nurse at Windsor's King Edward VII Hospital. One look at the child's pustular eruptions sufficed. She immediately had Andrew seen by a consultant who, at the sight of the multiple lesions, referred him to the government's dermatologist.

As a result of the consultation, his condition improved rapidly, and the enervating itching of the sero-purulent clusters ceased. I had to bathe the child in a permanganate solution and change his cotton pyjamas twice a day. Yet, despite these ministrations, our son remained in good spirits and enjoyed being whisked around in the buggy.

Whilst even an infectious skin disease, however worrying for a parent, hardly qualifies to be listed under 'Scares', Andrew had already caused us some real frights in the past, and he would continue the trend for some years to come.

We were still living in College Road when he caused us great anxiety one night. Suffering from tonsillitis and running a high temperature, he suddenly went into convulsions and passed out.

Although I suspected that they were a febrile reaction, I could not be sure that they did not signal something more serious. Before I had a chance to sketch the worst scenario, I alerted my husband, who, with the child in his arms and myself in tow, raced down the road to the Roman Catholic Hospital. Here, our request for help was met with the unblinking *sangfroid* of the reception nun who insisted on our first making a down payment, either in cash or by cheque, towards admission of the patient or any first aid to be rendered.

My husband, who during our hasty departure from our flat had left both his wallet and chequebook behind, cursed the hospital's money-oriented definition of charity. 'Surely, this is an emergency,' he screamed. But the Cerberus behind her glass partition pointed calmly to a notice which stated the terms of admission – there was no mention of any overriding action in the case of emergencies. Disgusted at the unchristian stance of a church-run institution, and with time now ticking noisily away, we fled back into the street.

In the chilly night air Andrew regained consciousness. As there was no taxi in sight I approached a car whose driver was about to leave the hospital grounds.

'Please,' I cried, 'would you take us to Kowloon General Hospital? Our son is very ill.'

The driver did not ask any questions. Neither did he ask for money. He was, well, just a good Samaritan.

'Of course,' he said, and opened the car door.

At the Government hospital Andrew was seen by a doctor straight away, and his blood and spinal fluid were tested for meningitis and other infectious, notifiable diseases.

How slowly the hours are passing when the health or life of one's child is hanging in the balance! How every minute multiplies and anxiety grows elephantine. Hours of waiting, in which a parent seems to be standing at the edge of an unfathomable chasm, either pleading with a personal god or beseeching the icons of technical advance and medical expertise.

Hours, aeons later, the results came back. Having tested negative for a critical infection, Andrew was suitably medicated and restored to his parents' care. I don't know how often I got up during the rest of the night to check up on the patient.

And now, as the years are sliding back, I am reminded of the day when, barely two years old, Andrew had caused me another moment of panic.

The children and I were spending the last day before our departure from Berlin at the British families' swimming pool in the grounds of the Olympic Stadium. While I was busy changing his baby brother's nappies, Andrew's early penchant for independence made him waddle off behind my back. Perhaps a minute passed before I felt a strange sensation creeping down my neck, telling me that something was wrong. As I turned around, I saw Andrew struggling in the children's pool, going under and not coming up again. Still fully dressed, I sprinted into the knee-high water whose slimy, slippery bottom slowed down my rescue attempt. And now common sense, if not instinct, dictated my action. Having pulled the toddler up, I slung his inert body over my shoulder, head down, depressed his tongue and slapped his back. It worked. As he came to, he coughed, spewed water and was soon breathing normally again. Yet only minutes later, while his tears were drying, the little rascal explored our luncheon basket. He was hungry. His mind had already discarded the incident. Mine, however, had not. Despite the warm sunshine I felt a cold wind rushing through me, as I reluctantly scripted a different outcome had it not been for that prickly sense of foreboding. Perhaps it made me admonish Andrew for his exploit in terms of love, rather than anger.

As he grew up, Andrew seemed to make a habit of going missing. At the age of three his desire for solo adventures made him disappear one day from our flat in Perth Street. Following an hour of frantic searching, his father eventually located him across the road on a building site, squatting with Chinese labourers and partaking of their lunch.

Two years later, while on our second three-year posting, and having just returned from inter-tour UK leave, Andrew took his life in his hands. We were now living in a first-floor flat in Dunbar Road, which backed on to the Perth Street officers' housing complex and came with a walled-in backyard. One afternoon the five-year-old and his sibling were being looked after by a friend of mine while I was visiting our eldest in hospital on Hong Kong Island. (While allegedly jumping a little too boisterously on a school trampoline, John had broken his arm and sustained a nasty bump on his head.) When, later that afternoon, I returned to pick up his brothers from the sixth-floor army flat in Kowloon Tsai, I found my friend close to hysterics. Andrew had absconded. In Army terms he had gone AWOL; in police terms he was 'missing'. 'One moment he was playing contentedly,' the mother of two wailed, 'the next one he was gone.'

Subsequent accounts did not make for easy listening. I barely took in that neighbours had helped to search the building and adjoining premises, and that the police had scanned the area around the nearby reservoir in which, not long ago, a Chinese toddler had drowned.

Once again a nightmare of emotions assailed me, spreading dread through my guts. As I walked the mile and a half back to our house, looking into every corner, behind every shrub, and expecting to hear the sound of an ambulance any minute, I once again implored the heavens – as mothers do in similar circumstances, whatever their beliefs.

But there was no sign of Andrew.

As I opened the door to our backyard, my demons of angst metamorphosed into cherubs of joy. For here, the subject of a major search operation was happily constructing a den with rattan chairs and a blanket. The little escapee greeted me with an innocent smile. 'Look, Mummy, I've built myself a house.'

Now, apart from explaining the foolishness of his behaviour, how could I possibly punish him? Instead, I hugged him and admired his building skill. Yet to this day it remains a mystery to me how, having never walked the route before, he had not only found his way down from the high-rise flat and into the busy street, but also across several side streets; how he had safely negotiated a large traffic roundabout, before locating the entrance to our close. Furthermore, on not finding anybody at home and the doors locked (it was the amah's day off), he had managed to climb into the backyard over a high, partly glass-spiked wall without suffering a single scratch. I am sure his guardian angel had taken him by the hand, but had that angel also lifted him over the wall?

I am happy to report that, following his flight from Kowloon Tsai, and with school about to impose its own timetable of activities, Andrew's enterprising spirit soon found other outlets.

How I Ended Up in Court

Once the children attended nursery school, I felt a need not only to earn some pocket money but also to expand intellectually. I tutored an English A-level student in German Literature, helping him to interpret the symbolism in Goethe's *Faust*. I also accepted a three-month 'professorship' at a Methodist College, teaching German to second-year Chinese students while the British incumbent of the post was on UK leave. As this was my first teaching job, I furiously revised German grammar and worked out a syllabus that would prevent students from dozing off during class. I am happy to say that I managed to keep my sophomores wide awake. But then they were keen to learn, and they would always bombard me with questions about Germany after each session. Delightfully polite, they were also immaculately turned out. All of them were of the Methodist faith.

This brief teaching spell came with a few fringe benefits. For within a short time I acquired a lively didactic and rhetorical skill which would twenty-five years later help me to face large audiences as a lecturer in the UK and abroad. It was also a chance to communicate with young studious Chinese whose bows and smiles acknowledged my teaching efforts.

For a while I worked as a part-time locum administrative secretary in the offices of the German director of the Lutheran World Federation of Churches, Herr Stumpf. Having lived in Peking as the Federation's representative for many years, he had fled the Chinese Cultural Revolution and set up a new head office in Kowloon. His aim was to support the local cottage industry – primarily the many Chinese refugees adept at making dolls and

63

Author at her desk as LWF administrative secretary

other craft items likely to find buyers in West Germany. All proceeds would then be used for the financial support of the artisans. Towards this end I was photographed with two Chinese children and dolls crafted by local refugees, to feature in a LWF pamphlet.

My duties were manifold. I translated documents, wrote letters in German or English and, as a local LWF representative, was once invited to a dinner given by the Hong Kong Soroptimist International. For the first time I came across women of all creeds and races, who had made it to the top of their careers. I remember I felt very small 'professionally', and never more desirous of further widening my mental horizon. It also opened my eyes to a group of people who were non-racist, humanitarian and charity-oriented, as well as tolerant of each other's faith.

My credentials as a translator and interpreter, plus a spot of good luck, soon landed me freelancing work for Hong Kong lawyers. I translated legal dispositions, decrees nisi and documents relating

Photograph of author for Lutheran World Federation
Hong Kong craft brochure

To Promote Goods Made By Refugees

Mrs Marianne Mackinnon, new Administrative Secretary of the Welfare Crafts Department of the Lutheran World Service, was presented to a group of Hongkong Soroptimists yesterday by Mrs Ellen Swan.

Mrs Mackinnon, who was born in Berlin, said that part of her work would be publicising, through correspondence in German, Hongkong products made by refugees.

She said that the fine craftsmanship in regard to gold and silver flatwork embroideries that was becoming almost obsolete in Hongkong, had been given new impetus through the influx of refugees during the past year.

Now that Chinese needlewomen, allowed to register in the Colony, have gone to Lutheran centres seeking welfare help, they are being given special training to use their old skills through a new medium.

The exquisite workmanship, so much a feature of the traditional Chinese wedding gowns, will now be seen on opera and theatre coats worn by women in the world's largest cities.

to commercial and civil law in cases involving German-speaking clients. To begin with, this proved to be painstaking work, since I first had to acquaint myself with the respective terminology. I would borrow books from the local library and, in a high-speed teach-yourself course, machete my way through the linguistic jungle of litigation. It was a time when singleness of mind was of the essence. Yet, though I was not yet dancing on the floor of judicial jargon, I was deftly moving along, in the process earning the respect and *viva-voce* recommendation of the Hong Kong legal fraternity. Word must also have spread through the corridors of the Hong Kong business and diplomatic community, for soon requests for translations came in from commercial companies, the *South China Economic Review* and the German Consulate.

The children would be peacefully asleep and my husband gently snoring while I was often still bent over my typewriter. Through the open windows of the Chinese apartments opposite there invariably drifted the clatter of shuffled mah-jong tiles. It would make me aware that there were other people defying the onslaught of the night.

My efforts bore fruits. Orders for translations were now coming in regularly and, one day, the Supreme Court Registrar appointed me as a freelance interpreter for criminal cases brought against German, Swiss or Austrian nationals, as well as for the odd juvenile court trial for attempted rape and other offences. The post, though, came with one slight drawback for courtroom novices like myself in that interpreters could not be told the nature of an indictment before the hearing, thus preventing me from familiarising myself in advance with the terminology appropriate to the charge.

During my first case I was still skating on thin ice, particularly during cross-examinations by the public prosecutor, who, instead of darting his barrage of questions at the defendant, would aim them straight at me, the interpreter – an awkward custom which made me feel as if I were in the dock. Slowly, practice, and the donning of a mental armoured jacket, boosted my confidence.

One case stands out for me: the indictment of a young German tourist whom Customs had caught trying to smuggle gold bullions out of the Colony. Valued at millions of HK dollars, they were found strapped to his body, cached in customised pockets of a corset. However, the choice of carrier had been a grave mistake by the men behind the crime, as the affected corpulence around the German's midriff was at odds with his otherwise gaunt looks and spindly physique, a sight which had struck Customs officials as strangely disproportionate and, ergo, suspect. Having been freed of his heavy encumbrance, the defendant claimed to have acted under intimidation. 'They threatened to kill me if I went to the police,' he cried, though he freely admitted that on safe arrival of the goods in London he would have been handsomely rewarded.

It looked as if it were going to be a lengthy trial.

Proceedings were in their second week when, one morning before dawn, I received a telegram from a Berlin hospital, advising me that my mother was seriously ill. Through MoD channels my husband immediately arranged for me to fly out that same evening by Army charter. As I was scheduled to be in court that morning, I decided to attend and ask the judge to relieve me from my present assignment.

Emotionally preoccupied, I needed a special effort during cross-examination that day, in order to concentrate and hit the right linguistic nuances. At the end of the hearing, and before the court adjourned for lunch, I asked to address the Judge. 'Your Honour,' I began and went on to inform him of my imminent departure and the need for a substitute interpreter.

The judge was suitably sympathetic. 'Tell the defendant that I shall give instructions to appoint another interpreter, so that the case may continue.'

The defendant now grew very agitated. He wrung his hands and, like a child robbed of its favourite toy, beseeched the judge to retain my services. 'I want her as my interpreter,' he cried, pointing a finger at me. 'I'll gladly wait in prison until she's back.'

Counsel smiled. So did the nonplussed judge, as with an air of amusement he adjourned the trial until such a time as Mrs MacKinnon would return. Flattering though the defendant's request had been, I felt uncomfortable at the notion that he might think that my German roots might tempt me to phrase his statements so subtly as to favourably influence the outcome of the trial.

Two weeks later I was back in Hong Kong, greatly relieved that my mother's life no longer hung in the balance and that I had been able to see her settled back at home. On my return to court, the defendant greeted me like a long-lost friend. Yet when the judge finally pronounced sentence, there was no leniency, impartial as I had remained in my verbal rendition at all times.

Turning towards me, thunder and lightning in his eyes and voice, the young man in the dock spat his anger at me, the woman he had presumed would save him out of fellow-feelings for a compatriot. But then he would have three years during which to muse about the professionalism of a German-born court interpreter and British citizen.

How I Held Up Mongolian Raiders

One of the oddest experiences I had during my stay in Hong Kong was of my own making.

I had been engaged as a part-time translator and synopsis writer by Shaw Brothers Film Studios, the largest Chinese film company in the Far East at the time. On my first day in office I went to explore the location during my lunch break, a banana in my hand. Unchallenged, I passed gorgeous sets of palaces and temples, lavishly robed courtiers and concubines of some Tang, Ming or Manchu emperor, peasants in rags, warriors engaged in awe-inspiring sword play, and other players in an industry that brings make-believe to the Chinese screen.

An empty studio invited me to investigate further. However, the plethora of cables, light and sound equipment held little interest for me, so instead I went out at the other end into what looked like a replica of a medieval village street, lined with the façades of one-storeyed mock-wooden cabins. There was no one about and it was as eerily quiet as the town in Hollywood's *High Noon*.

I was about to peel my banana when there came the sudden thunder of hooves. Seemingly from nowhere, a cavalcade of wild-looking Mongol riders appeared at the far end, brandishing scimitars, and with stomach-churning cries on their lips. As they galloped down the street towards me, their shaggy horses whirled up clouds of dust.

Like a flash of lightning a history lesson shot through my mind. Surely these were the Mongol hordes of Genghis Khan, the infamous barbarian warrior who had brought unimaginable terror to Central Asia in the thirteenth century; who had come, indeed, to the very gates of Europe? And here I stood, a twentieth-century lady in a knee-length blue-and-white frock, frozen to the spot and holding up a half-peeled banana like a flickering candle!

But now, regardless of my presence, the upstairs windows in the 'street' suddenly opened and buckets of a viscous, yellow fluid were emptied over the invaders. Screams of pain cleaved the air, before the oil-drenched advance party came to an abrupt halt. Horses reared and neighed, camera crews emerged, the riders stared. Shouts. The director's shrill voice jerked me out of my trance. First in Cantonese, then with a Hollywood expletive – the ultimate send-off: 'What the hell, woman...?'

I turned on my heels and as fast as I could returned to the safety of my office, wondering how to explain my unscripted appearance on set.

Although I got reprimanded by one of the Shaw brothers, albeit lightly, I noted with a frisson of shame that I had cost the company more than a hatful of Hong Kong dollars. For now the light was no longer right for a retake, the horses had to be watered and the buckets of 'hot oil' refilled, while technicians restored the ghost-town look of the set. Only the extras, the horsemen, grinned in anticipation of another day's shooting, since this would boost their take-home pay.

I am glad to say that I did not get the chance to hold up another historic ambush, nor to crash into some imperial court scene or distract a would-be assassin from dealing with his victim in the fashion of the time. For I resigned at the end of the month. As the only white European woman in the Hong Kong studios of Shaw Brothers' vast movie-making empire, I felt unashamedly, yet explicably, out of place.

I forget what happened to my banana that day.

Voices of Childhood

I must begin by asking for the reader's indulgence. For here I intend recalling some of the artless, humorous and often poignant utterances of my children – what the Germans often call *Kindermund*. 'Out of the mouths of babes...' they say. Some of these utterances, in particular, planted themselves firmly in my mind and time has not erased them. They can still make me smile and – in the words of threepenny romantic novels – warm the cockles of my heart.

A German poet said once that our children are only totally and unconditionally ours 'within the narrow realm of their childhood': those precious years in which we should love them and have them love us. The emphasis is on *love*. We must treasure those short

Author with children on Hong Kong Peak

years and, if so blessed, store them in our mind's archive like priceless memorabilia.

I remember it was Mother's Day when the poet's lines came to my mind. The morning when the three boys tiptoed into the bedroom and woke me with a peck each on my cheek. 'Happy Mother's Day,' they whispered, trying not to wake their father. Coloured cards depicting smiling suns, flowers and three manikins, and carrying the boys' names, landed on my duvet, together with a spray of pretty little wild blooms which they must have picked from the empty site opposite. Forgetting Father's need for rest, John now went and started playing a Czerny sonata on the piano, while Andrew, who had recently finished the Janet and John series of Enid Blyton's Ladybird books, tried to read out the headlines of the morning paper. Donald, meanwhile, not wanting to be outdone by his brothers, fetched a mug of tea from the amah and carried it to my bed as if there were a prize for not spilling its content.

Andrew, despite being a little rascal with a flair for independent actions, frequently made me laugh and sometimes caused me an emotional flutter. One day he announced: 'Me and my girlfriend we fell in love. We kissed on the lips. Her name is Mary-Ann. I am going to marry her.' I forgot whether I felt a twinge of jealousy.

I remember the morning when three little girls from his first year at school appeared at the door, wanting to play with him. 'What do you want to play?' I asked. 'The kissing game,' they replied. Intrigued I probed further. 'Why do you want to play this game?' The answer was unequivocal. 'Because we love Andrew.' With a bemused smile, the subject of the young ladies' infatuation followed them outside 'to play'.

One day he told me that he was running a secret club. 'So far I've got only one member,' he revealed. 'Me.' And questioned as to the exclusivity of the club, he explained, 'Because I can't trust anyone else.' Well, with his popularity further in ascendance, it was not long before several keen cubs applied for membership.

I have never forgotten the day he brought me a beautiful hibiscus flower, stealthily picked, I presume, from a neighbour's garden.

'For you, Mummy,' he said, putting his arms around my neck. 'Aaaah', the reader will say, but the subsequent statement made that gesture of affection yet more poignant: 'I'm so happy to have a mummy, not like some other children who haven't.' I never queried what had prompted such an observation.

Andrew quickly picked up some Cantonese from Aho, and during the Christmas season would greet every Chinese with '*Kung Hoi Fat Choi*', the equivalent of 'Happy New Year'.

John, our eldest, I remember as a quiet, patient and studious child. He was learning to play the piano with a former German concert pianist, and regularly received prizes in school for reading and writing, as well as for tidiness and politeness. He would help me carry shopping bags and tell his brothers to put their toys away at night. When he started to play tennis, he was so enamoured with his racquet that he wanted to take it to bed. He was also very affectionate, though in an unobtrusive way. One day – I can't remember why the subject of death and dying came up – he put his arms around me and said, 'I hope you won't die, Mummy.'

Anyone for tennis?

73

On another occasion, when he was seven or eight – oh, how children's words stay anchored in a mother's mind! – he looked at me, dressed up as I was to go to a ball with his father, and said: 'You look as pretty as a princess.' Well, what mother's heart would not beat faster at hearing such a compliment from the mouth of her son? What mother in her twilight years, or living in the penumbra of lonesome old age, would not remember similarly poignant comments with a smile?

Christmas, of course, was a particularly wonderful time, even if it was celebrated in bright sunshine and European spring temperatures, and without bell-ringing, carolling and the scent of a 'real' tree. There was still turkey with all the trimmings on the table, we still pulled crackers and wore silly hats, and the children unwrapped their presents as excitedly as they would have back home. On Easter Sunday, the venue for the children's Easter egg hunt was the living room, while birthday parties featured sausage rolls, candles on an iced cake, crisps and sweets, as well as all the fun of 'musical chairs' and other games. While the expat community often readily

Life on an island beach

74

Children playing on the beach

adapted to local conditions, most families continued to live by their own standards and Western customs.

A host of other priceless images remain: afternoons by the swimming pool or on some idyllic island beach. Walks through Kowloon's hinterland of tangled vegetation, past antedeluvian boulders and dried-up water channels. On one such ramble my husband had to dispose of a waylaying, nasty-looking snake. He did so in true golfer's style, by using a long stick as he would tee off with a No. 1 wood. As in a slide show I see us visiting villages, where Hakka women in fabric-draped, wok-shaped hats worked in paddy fields or on vegetable plots; hamlets alive with roaming children, chickens and mongrel dogs. And for its sheer exotic allure, I recall the vibrancy of the local markets. Other pictures conjured up with ease are the children riding their cycles in our close: playing cowboys and Indians, making music and participating in swimming contests. Sometimes they would bring

Author's husband disposing of waylaying snake

Author with children

home strange objects in glasses, and once a stray cat. I'm afraid the feline enjoyed only a short home life on account of its habit of urinating on the living room carpet, which did not amuse Aho and left a most undesirable stench in the room.

Looking back over those years, I realise how fortunate I was to be able to live with my sons through 'the realms of their childhood'. To have had the privilege of motherhood, and to have been allowed to love them and to be loved in return; to see them growing up and developing into loveable, responsible adults capable themselves of loving and caring. Furthermore, to have had the time – and the wisdom – to tell them about things that are not being taught in nurseries and schools, and of which we adults speak as 'hovering between heaven and earth'.

Lantao Island

In the summer of 1962 the heat reached record temperatures. Twenty-five per cent of the Chinese refugees, who lived one family to a room in the beehive tower-block flats of the resettlement schemes, were reported to be sleeping in the streets at night. Air-conditioned cinemas had full houses, as they promised a temporary escape from the heat. To make the situation worse, the continuing drought augured ill for the Colony's water supply. With reservoir levels at their lowest for decades, it was rumoured that the daily two-hour domestic supply would soon be cut to a twice-weekly one.

The hut (1963) on mountain saddle of Fu-Shan

In our bedrooms, which did not enjoy the luxury of air conditioners, ceiling fans droned away day and night, but brought about no more than the zephyr-like relief of a hand-held Chinese fan. The children, though, seemed to take the heat in their stride. However, with restful sleep virtually impossible, my husband found it difficult to get through a day's work at the office. And so, as the hothouse heat increasingly tore at the adults' nerves, he decided to take a ten-day holiday.

Rather than 'hopping' over to Tokyo, the long-weekend destination favoured by many expatriates, we rented a six-bunk, crofter-style cottage on Lantao Island from the Methodist Mission, one of several such dwellings scattered across the saddle of the 3,000-feet Fu Shan

Author's husband with children

80

Author in front of hut

mountain. Its location promised pure, cooler air in exchange for a
basic lifestyle away from urban civilisation. It also offered unequalled
views across the sea to the surrounding islands and mainland China.

We travelled to the island by hovercraft, the vessel needling its
way through a chain of small islands, and through waters infested
with large-tasselled jellyfish. From Lantao pier a single, narrow
footpath led up the jagged, scrub-covered mountain. Although, by
now, the sun was close to its zenith and the heat was bearing down
on us, Donald walked sturdily ahead, as if to give early notice that
he intended to become a rock climber in later life. I, however,
soon felt as if I were scaling the steps of the Eiffel Tower, while
my husband, equally unused to physical exercise, called for frequent
stops, in order to catch his breath. He did not speak, and I began
to wonder whether he was querying the wisdom of opting for our
chosen holiday location.

Ablutions outside the hut

Spring water mountain swimming pool

Nevertheless, we continued to plot on, sweat leaking from every pore. From time to time the children would call out, 'Come on, Daddy; come on, Mummy', whenever their progenitors lagged too far behind. Sometimes, Donald, leader of the troupe, would look down on the stragglers as if he were guiding an advance party up Mount Everest. Now and then, we stopped at a stream, greedily scooping up the crystal-clear water in our hand, wetting our parched throats and cooling our faces. Finally, at the end of a two-hour climb, we reached the saddle underneath the grassy knoll of Fu Shan.

Our sparsely furnished accommodation promised no-star unsophisticated living. Apart from an outsize chemical toilet, it came with oil lamps and a butane gas cylinder for the one-ring cooker. A meagre stream of water ran from the roof tank, through a single pipe and into a small kitchen sink. We had, indeed, exchanged an urban lifestyle for one bereft of modern conveniences.

The saddle (other huts in the background)

It was a challenge, one that rewarded the holidaymaker with oh, so breathable, bracing air.

In the absence of a bathroom, our ablutions took place outside the hut in view of the rising sun as it cast pink hues over the peak before exploding within minutes into an all-embracing intense light. A tub of water, placed on a chair, served as a wash basin. Breakfast was eggs and bacon, and for supper I would serve sizzling sausages with tinned accompaniments – simple standby meals taken al fresco at a table hewn out of sheer rock. As we ate, below us were priceless vistas that extended out across the sea, dotted here and there with a lone sampan or fishing boat.

The provision of food for breakfast and supper presented no problem. Each day coolies would carry up basic groceries on long poles, as ordered by the individual families, and by the two Bostonian anthropologists on a working holiday who ran the communal hut and cooked a daily American-style lunch for the 'campers'.

During the day the children enjoyed paddling in a large spring-fed pool, searching for tadpoles, baby crabs, salamanders and frogs, while Andrew, our naturalist, forever equipped with empty jam jars, collected grasshoppers, beetles and strange objects of a botanical or geological nature. Several huge boulders, strewn around the mountain saddle in some prehistoric stellar or volcanic cataclysm, provided the children with targets to climb, draw or hide behind, while the grassy mat of the saddle doubled up as a safe playground.

In the evenings, while their father was relishing a cool beer in the communal hut, I sometimes took the children outside to look at the night sky. I particularly recall one such night: a widescreen, star-sequinned and seemingly infinite black void, in which a giant full moon was bathing the whole of our plateau in a wan light, lending everything in it an enthralling, magical intensity. 'Where does God live? And what lies behind the stars?' the children might ask, and my tentative answers, full of the wonders and the Unknown of the Universe, would accompany them to bed.

Alas, our brief respite from Hong Kong's scorching summer ended all too soon. Now, well over forty-five years later, I hate

Lantao 'floating village'

to think what Lantao Island might look like today. Will the sleepy, time-struck village of Tai O at the foot of Fu Shan, the beached sampans, the shacks on stilts, the market, and the creek which admitted no more than a trickle of water at high tide, have given way to a multi-storey housing development? Will planners have made the saddle and peak of 'our' mountain more accessible to day trippers, by building a concrete road or a funicular tram to a panoramic restaurant? Will the pristine sandy beach at Silvermine Bay now be the sunbathing territory of loud-mouthed, ghetto-blasting lager tourists? Will the impressive monastery at Po Lin, which we visited on another occasion by courtesy of the Abbot, and which was then reached by water taxi and a steep path on the eastern side of the island, have become just another tourist attraction? Perhaps monks were now charging for a glass of milk and demanding a donation or an entrance fee to their grounds and holy chapel.

I am glad I don't know. Indeed, I do not want to know. The memory of the mountain saddle of Fu Shan, as well as of the beautiful hills and valleys of Lantao Island, to which subsequent outings took us, dwell unspoilt in my mind.

Typhoon 'Mary'

Whilst living in Hong Kong we experienced two typhoons which went on record as being among the most destructive. For anyone used to a temperate climate they were certainly scary spectacles of nature. We lived through them as through a nightmare.

Occurring mainly during the monsoon season, these powerful storms often had a lethal impact on the Colony's urban areas, as well as its island and mainland villages. They would sweep across with a ferocious energy, and with no respect for anything that could be torn loose, splintered or lifted out of the water and onto land. At least once during our expat years a storm caused a tsunami-like wave which exacted a high human toll.

I remember Typhoon Wanda as a top-graded storm which raked over roofs and through streets with a leonine roar. At its height, the children and I huddled together in the depth of the living room, away from the windows and the threat of blown-in shards of glass. We watched anxiously as objects flew past or thudded against the windows, and as the bamboo scaffolding on the Chinese block of flats opposite was reduced to a heap of matchsticks within minutes. A builders' canvas sheet took to the air like a kite, as did anything that could be whirled up and tossed around. Telephone lines were down. There was no delivery of milk or groceries, no newspapers and no public transport. Its main cable being damaged, Radio Hong Kong now operated on an emergency transmitter.

Twenty-four hours later the first details of the storm's ravages came to light. Ships had foundered while many smaller vessels and private yachts had been hoisted out of the harbour and hurled ashore. Cranes had tumbled; motor cars had piled up in the streets.

Many lives were said to have been lost when at high tide a huge wave had swept ashore, burying a whole fishing village under its onslaught. In urban areas, torrential rain had left its own signature: sewers were overflowing, popping grilles and spewing out rats. For a few days there was a state of emergency. Life as we had known it came to a standstill.

Unfortunately this violent storm did not remain our only experience of the destructive force of nature. Two years later my husband and I got caught in Typhoon Mary at the peak of its incursion. Not because we had acted unwisely or with a lack of circumspection, but because – like many other local residents – we were misled by Radio Hong Kong's half-hourly weather reports, according to which the storm was said to be veering away from the Colony and likely to spend itself outwith its waters.

It was the last day of August, allegedly the hottest and driest month since 1925, and my husband and I had decided to go to the cinema. Admittedly, it was quite windy, but having been reassured about the weather, we left the children in the care of our trusted amah. As it turned out, it was the only time in many years that the weathermen were taken by surprise. For, in a sudden U-turn, the storm changed direction again and headed back towards Hong Kong and the mainland, being upgraded to hurricane force. There was little time for ships to leave the harbour and ride out the storm at sea, nor for smaller vessels to seek the relative safety of the typhoon shelter.

Of all this my husband and I, like the rest of the cinema audience, were blissfully unaware. By the time we left, a Force 12 storm was charging through the streets, dislodging anything unable to withstand its ferocity. Glass, street signs and sheet metal were flying through the air horizontally, each a potential guillotine. Scaffolding was crashing down, lengths of cables were whipping the air like a cat o' nine tails.

My husband, who in World War II had been a member of the first British Expeditionary Force and taken prisoner at St Valéry-Sur-Somme off the French coast, ignored the inherent danger of venturing out into the streets. 'Let's try and get home to the children,' he said, and I agreed, fearing that they might be upset by the cacophony and mayhem outside. It may have been foolish to pitch human determination against the raging elements, but how does parental concern measure against the odds?

We set off along the flooded street towards Nathan Road, keeping as close as possible to the side of buildings, each of us holding over our head a piece of ripped-off soggy cardboard like a coolie hat in the naive hope that it might protect us against lethal airborne objects.

Drenched to the skin, and buffeted by gusts that flattened us to walls or propelled us forward, we reached our car. Miraculously, no tree had fallen on it or smashed the windscreen; miraculously, too, it started. But now the tentative drive along the thoroughfare, which by now resembled an obstacle course strewn with the storm's debris, required daredevil skill. With all the street lights gone, visibility was down to zero, except for the diluted beam of the car's headlights and, briefly, for the scattered light of a fire engine whose team was trying to shift what looked like the crown of a tree, but which could have been any other obstacle barricading the road. My husband had no choice: he drove the car on to the pavement and snaked it forward. The rain was drumming on the roof of the car, branches slashed against the windows, sometimes obscuring the driver's vision. Ducking on the back seat, adrenalin-high, I half expected our car to be hit and flattened any minute. 'Lie down flat,' shouted my husband, when something heavy landed on the boot. I complied. I felt helpless and, literally, at the mercy of the elements. Memories flashed back to February 1945, to the carpet-bombing of Berlin. To naked fear rummaging in my guts every time I heard bombs whistling on their way down, before thumping home and exploding with a dull, oppressive sound. I had felt helpless then – and, like an ant or fly, dispensable...

But now, at last, a recognisable landmark: our street, our house. Sighs of relief. Apart from the car's dents and bruises we had won our war.

A worried Aho came to meet the rain-soaked and dishevelled parents who rushed into the children's bedroom.

There, our three angels were peacefully asleep.

People I Have Met

My work with the German Consulate invariably brought me into contact with the kind of people I might normally not have met. Here, two German VIPs, to whom I was delegated as an interpreter and hostess, head the list.

One, whom Consulate officials introduced as 'Herr Schmidt', did not strike me as a man of the common breed. He was middle-aged, slim, soft-spoken and impeccably dressed, and his manners were those of a gentleman of the old school. With his finely sculptured features and a high forehead he reminded me of a magazine picture I had seen of a Hohenzollern prince at a high-society wedding. Herr Schmidt's business in Hong Kong was, however, very much down to earth. He was the representative of a well-known German shoe manufacturer, hoping to promote the company's lines in the Far East. In broader terms, he was – or seemed to be – no more than a travelling salesman. From the start, however, I suspected that 'Schmidt' was not his real name, and the bowing and scraping of some lower Consular officials confirmed to me that there was indeed a diplomatic 'cover-up'.

This mysterious gentleman was staying at the palatial Mandarin Hotel, where his suite served as a mini showroom for the hundreds of shoes which he had brought with him to display to potential Chinese importers. Yet I soon noticed that he lacked the patter and persuasive mannerisms of the bona fide salesman. I suppose he was unable to deal with potential buyers with less than all the attributes of good breeding. Nothing pointed more markedly to his being an aristocrat than two silver-framed photographs on display in his hotel room: one showing a grand castle on a hill, the other a bejewelled lady wearing a ball gown and a tiara. Yet when asked about the location of the castle, Herr Schmidt merely explained that it stood in what was now East Germany, whereupon his face closed up and good manners forbade me from probing any further.

A visit to a local fabric shop provided more food for my suspicion. Without any bargaining whatsoever he bought several full lengths of heavy silk and taffeta for his wife, suitable for grand occasions. He might have lost his castle, I thought, but back home, somewhere in West Germany or West Berlin, he might still be one of the stars of German high society, an aristocrat whom the war, like many other members of the German nobility, had reduced to earning his living like any Tom, Dick or Harry; in fact like any ordinary Herr Schmidt. At the end of his stay he invited me for a drink at the hotel bar and delicately handed me what he called 'an appreciation of my services'.

Another VIP, though of a different social calibre, brushed my life as Consular interpreter. I shall refer to him as Mr X.

A partner in what was then West Germany's largest radio and

Author at VIP cocktail party

television manufacturing company, Herr X was visiting Hong Kong on a promotional tour. Given VIP status by the German Consulate, he stayed at the Hilton Hotel, where full courtesies were extended to him. Yet Herr X was the most blasé, most ungracious man I had ever come across. I took an instant dislike to him. Hong Kong radio and TV dealers, on the other hand, on the lookout for some lucrative business, fêted him like a commercial superstar.

Conscious of his company's international standing, Herr X took any accolades in his stride, never conceding favours, and never with more than a tired smile acknowledging Chinese courtesies. His English was negligible, and the paucity of phrases suggested that he had never learnt it at school. I interpreted for him at a press conference at the Hilton Hotel, at dinners given by British and Hong Kong company directors and at various business meetings, but whatever the function his demeanour always implied that he saw himself as someone of iconic stature and as such was bored by all the underlings he had to deal with. Perhaps he had somehow forgotten that he had started out rather humbly, so I was told, as a small-time dealer in scrap metal.

Author at press conference

One morning I accompanied him in the air-conditioned Hilton limousine on a sightseeing trip around Hong Kong Island, the kind of courtesy tour which offered breathtaking views of the harbour and outlying islands, half-hidden, conifer-backed sandy coves and sandy beaches, a scenery made for cameras and painting brushes. However, Herr X showed no interest in the exquisite tableaux we were passing. Indeed, judging by his expression, he might just as well have been travelling past his former industrial scrapyards.

Despite this affected indifference, he celebrated his birthday in the Colony in style. Here now was his opportunity to show off his company's standing and – no expense spared – to make his mark on Hong Kong's commercial landscape. For his birthday party he hired the Hilton yacht, a luxury craft moored at Blake pier and made for leisurely jaunts through the harbour or cruises to neighbouring islands. The vessel carried a Chinese crew, while the Hilton's chef was in charge of the gourmet catering.

Herr X's secretary, a man in his thirties, who looked as if he were suffering from consumption or a stress-induced stomach ulcer, handled the guest list, which included myself, as well as some stunningly beautiful Chinese party girls. Food was brought aboard on silver platters and in steamers. Waiters in white served champagne, someone played the accordion and conversation flowed agreeably between the coloured lights strung across the vessel. The harbour at night was in itself an experience. A flood of coloured lights ran up to the Peak and hugged the shorelines, while, here and there, the beacons of ships rippled on the dark water like fallen stars.

For me, the trip was a hedonistic treat. But for Herr X it was clearly only one more exotic morsel that barely registered on his supersaturated and jaded palate.

When he left Hong Kong, this surly, pompous gentleman, who had never once said 'please' or 'thank-you', and who in his dealings with his secretary had acted like a slave-driver, made me nurse a rather uncharitable thought. Seeing him off at the airport with a perfunctory smile, I barely repressed a cry of 'good riddance'. True to style, he did not leave me a tip.

A few months later I read in the *South China Morning Post* that, much to the embarrassment of the German Consulate, Herr X had been arrested in Germany for defrauding his partner and company shareholders of several million Deutschmarks. Following a lengthy court hearing, he was reported to have been sentenced to several years in jail. To this day I wonder how his inflated ego might have fared in a place where self-appointed royalty is quickly dethroned and dragged through the prison mire.

The President of the German Federal Republic, Heinrich Lübke, on a 'state visit' to the Colony, was another VIP I met. I shook hands with him and his wife, Wilhelmine, at a cocktail party hosted by the German Consulate. The event had mustered local government officials, the managing directors of German and British companies trading in Hong Kong, as well as the *crème de la crème* of Chinese residents.

It was fun to watch how, gently or none too gently, some elbowed their way into the President's inner circle, and how to others even Frau Wilhelmine's flabby hand seemed to confer status. Such a

Author at party with husband and the Hong Kong manager of Jardine & Matheson

congregation allowed me another good look at what constituted Hong Kong society, at people with whom I would normally not rub shoulders, and whose social values and aspirations were, ultimately, far removed from my own and those of my husband. As the wife of an intelligence officer, known in foreign postings as a 'dependant', my life was clearly staked within the social strata of the British Army community and, here again, within the even narrower confines of officers and their families. But then, how could I possibly be envious? I was the mother of three beautiful and loveable sons. They were my status symbol.

Members of the British Forces in Hong Kong, particularly intelligence officers and their families, had orders, I believe, not to befriend or employ local Chinese unless they had first been thoroughly security-vetted. We were not to forget that there was a constant influx of refugees from mainland China, and that Peking was known to filter Communist sympathisers and spies into the Colony. Thus, there existed an invisible no-go area in which the two cultures seldom met, except at government level, during official cocktail parties, in commerce and as British employers of office staff and servants.

Social pursuits within my husband's unit extended, therefore, no farther than official functions and the ubiquitous cocktail parties, at which the men would congregate at the bar, and the wives club together, discussing servants, the latest consignment of M&S children's clothes at a certain store, and the 'academic' achievements or antics of their little darlings.

In our circle of acquaintances Hans Li was the odd Chinese, yet notable exception. I forget how we met, but not what had initially attracted him to my family. Nor do I know what role he played in my husband's field of work. I never asked. Wives of intelligence officers never asked questions, wherever their overseas postings took them.

A white-collar Hong Kong-born man, Hans had been a pre-war

Hans Li and the author at a wedding reception

engineering graduate from Munich University, working in his postgraduate years on plans for the Munich underground railway. He was a lover of all things German and Bavarian – bar Hitler and the excesses of the Third Reich. Intrigued by the fact that I was German-born, he would bombard me with rusty German phrases, many of which had long disappeared from everyday use. He never tired of swooning over Bavaria's beautiful mountains, its beer served up in steins and the local bucolic *Lederhosen* culture. Many were the occasions when he proudly stated that he was 'almost' a German, and definitely a *Münchener*. When one of his relatives got married, he invited us to the lavish Cantonese-style wedding banquet, at the end of which, and before some musicians played Western tunes for dancing, the mother-of-the-bride handed envelopes to the guests for donations to the happy couple's trousseau.

He was also a very generous man. One day he picked us up in his Studebaker and drove us to his summer villa at Repulse Bay on Hong Kong Island. Here he and his friends entertained us as if we had presented our host with a crate of Bavarian beer or a genuine pair of *Lederhosen*. Sometimes his presents, which we were never able to match, rather embarrassed us. When, during one of her visits to the Colony, Hans met my mother, about whom everything was German and upper middle class, he insisted that the 'lady from Berlin' accept a striking red-and-gold silk jacket and black trousers. My mother, visibly unsure whether Chinese etiquette allowed her to decline the gift, finally accepted it with perfect grace and later reciprocated the honour by giving a lengthy description of life in Berlin in the thirties, under Hitler and during the war. It was of little consequence that she had never worn trousers before, nor ever would. For, eye-fetching as the outfit with the bold dragon design was, it would have no place in her wardrobe, used as the 67-year-old widow was to less conspicuous dress styles and muted colours. When she died, Mr Li's gift found its way into an Oxfam shop. Alas, it was two sizes too small for me.

At the end of our final tour, Hans' farewell present for me would be a white angora wool, pearl-embroidered cardigan. It, too, came to lead a virginal existence in my wardrobe. I forgot what became of it.

If only Hans had asked me for my dress size.

An invitation to dinner at the flat of the Chief Editor of the *South China Morning Post* was an occasion which for the length of an evening allowed my husband and me to meet some people whose intellectual *niveau* and knowledge of local and Far Eastern matters made for lively conversation. Laid for ten, the shiny, candlelit rosewood table was a feast for the eye. Heaving under the sparkle of silver and crystal, with a glass bowl of white roses as its centre-piece, it complemented the delectable dishes and the fine wines served by a maid in a lace-fringed cap and apron, and by a waiter of the stately butler kind. Having lived for the best part of twelve years in British Army G-Plan-furnished houses or flats, my senses revelled in the ambience, while I savoured the haute-cuisine food which was far removed from the traditional fare of an MoD family.

I was reminded of my grandmother's luncheon parties in the days before the war, which, if on a less opulent scale, had at least given me some grounding in the art of fine dining. Another memorable dinner also comes to mind. It was just a few months after the end of the war and I was living out of a small suitcase in an unheated furnished room in Lüneburg, West Germany, where I was working for a unit of the British Occupying Forces. One day I was surprised to receive an invitation to dinner from the officers of a Belgian detachment. For years I had been living on a near-starvation diet and the promise of a proper meal with all the trimmings seemed like a dream.

On the day of the dinner I was driven to a palatial mansion which, seized during the late 1930s from its Jewish owner by a Nazi official, had subsequently been requisitioned by the Belgian forces occupying a sector east of the river Elbe. In my faded Sunday dress – the only one which the war had left me – I felt like Cinderella. With a sense of wonder I surveyed the banquet-length table and tasted the various dishes prepared by a French chef.

I had to silence the warning voice in my head that the next morning I would have to return to my battle for personal survival. But what the hell, I thought, and for the next few hours I unashamedly enjoyed all the fun and pleasure the good life can offer.

I thought with gratitude of my French teacher at school who had ingrained in his pupils a solid French vocabulary, along with a passable command of irregular verbs; and I thanked my parents retrospectively for having taught me good table manners. Not wanting to appear greedy, I thus declined the offer of a third cream-topped blueberry tart, something I was to regret for days.

After dinner there was dancing to gramophone records in the splendid ballroom, a scaled-down version of Versailles' famous Hall of Mirrors. Attractively turned out in their dress uniforms, the officers slow-waltzed, foxtrotted or boogied the ladies around the floor to the sound of an American dance orchestra.

'*Mademoiselle?* ...'

An Innocent Abroad

In the spring of 1963 my mother visited us. She greatly enjoyed her stay, meeting our friends, including Hans Li and Herr Stumpf, each of whom would invite her and myself out to a gourmet lunch at Gaddi's. She surveyed with interest the intricacies of Chinese life and culture and with relish soaked up the Colony's picture-postcard views.

She was booked on a scheduled BOAC return flight to Frankfurt, from where she would fly across the Russian Zone back to Berlin.

Author's mother with her grandchildren in Dunbar Road

On the evening of her departure she was patiently waiting by her suitcase, whilst my husband fiddled with his black tie and I wrestled into my evening dress. For having once waved Mother goodbye at the airport, we planned to attend a ball at the United Services Club.

We left on time but at the check-in desk we were informed that the flight had already left; that all passengers had been notified of the aircraft's earlier departure, and that my mother, having turned up late, had thus forfeited her ticket. Our anger-fuelled arguments that we had not been contacted fell on deaf ears, so did our request for a refund or, preferably, a seat on the next flight to Germany. Our remonstrations were met with perfunctory smiles and the advice that we should contact the airline direct.

As deflated as punctured balloons at the end of a party, we returned home.

Author's mother and grandchildren on a sampan

Next day I took up the matter with the airline's office. But not until after I had ploughed my way past minor staff with negative attitudes did I reach management level and the promise of assistance.

A week went by, during which my mother unashamedly enjoyed

Author's mother and grandchildren waiting for Star Ferry

the unscheduled extension of her holiday. By now she had seen spectacular views, as well as – from afar – the pitiful shanties of refugees waiting for resettlement; she had shopped for jewellery, had a dress made from Thai silk, squeezed herself through narrow market lanes, watched Hakka women working in the rice fields and lounged on some idyllic beaches. The Star Ferry had become her favourite cross-harbour transport, and afternoon tea at the Peninsular Hotel the epitome of English colonial life. To add a

Author's mother in rickshaw

new experience to her prolonged stay, we took her by boat to Macao, the Portuguese colony famed for its casinos and its remnants of Hispanic architecture. We also took a photograph of her sitting in a red-and-gold rickshaw – an ancient form of transport that now mainly served as a tourist attraction and seldom ventured out into mainstream traffic.

Hans Li, who had earlier enjoyed a special Bavarian meal of sausages, smoked pork, dumplings, sauerkraut and imported beer at our flat, added another highlight to my mother's stay, by inviting all of us to dinner at Aberdeen's Floating Restaurant in the Boat People's Bay, a community of permanently moored sampans on Hong Kong Island. My husband and I chose a fish from a large tank for our *dim sum*, an option which my mother did not fancy, partial though she was to eating fish, though not to seeing it swimming happily first. However, she did not have to be asked twice to sit in an exquisitely crafted, throne-like chair which

Aberdeen's Floating Restaurant (from left: author's husband, Mrs Li, author's mother, Hans Li and author)

allegedly had once stood in Peking's Imperial Palace. Not surprisingly a photographer materialised to take a picture of our group.

In the meantime, my husband was pulling strings with the Army and MoD travel units, who had been acquainted with my mother's plight. Thus, when BOAC finally arranged for a free flight to Bangkok, the Army squeezed her on to a chartered Pacific Airways flight from the Thai capital to Amsterdam, whence she would have to make her own way back to Berlin. They did not tell her in what kind of company she would find herself.

The story of how my mother, on her return journey, coped with situations which she would not have envisaged in her dreams, and which had required her to be tolerant and adaptable in spirit, was to enliven conversation at parties and among her coterie of friends for years to come.

The flight to Bangkok, we were told, went without a hitch.

Miraculously, a taxi driver did not take advantage of the elderly lady and delivered her safely to a discreet hotel largely screened off from the onslaught of that vibrant city. Yet, once she had been given a room and had freshened herself up, she decided – most unwisely in view of the lateness of the hour – to go for a stroll around the block, to stretch her legs and tell folk back home what she had glimpsed of the Thai capital.

Her sightseeing tour was apparently short-lived, as she soon realised that a European woman walking the streets of Bangkok after nightfall makes her an easy target for a plethora of shady characters. I don't know what particular hazards or temptations she encountered, but she must have had a guardian angel, for she returned to the hotel feeling none the worse for her exploit, albeit a little shaken and out of breath and still clasping her handbag tightly. Her confidence must have taken a beating, though. Thus, instead of trying a restaurant or room service for a meal, she went to bed on the frugal fare of a BOAC apple and packet of biscuits.

The following morning, already feeling one step nearer to home, she presented herself at the airport. I can see her in my mind, wringing her hands in dismay, if not in shock, as she realised that she was the only female passenger among a planeload of Chinese seamen, a party of smiles, polite nods and muted sing-song talk. Yet, given a seat by herself, and with the stewardesses treating her like a VIP travelling incognito, she soon settled down to her new experience. The behaviour of the young mariners – crews on their way to joining their ships in Amsterdam – put her further at ease, as they showed her the kind of respect which, in their culture, they would have shown an elderly member of their family. 'They were so polite,' my mother would recall, 'and so neatly dressed!' What she equally enthused about was the pilot's invitation to view Kashmir and the rose-tinted foothills of the Hindu Kush from the cockpit at sunrise, and that she was served a German-style meal in lieu of sweet and sour pork and fried rice.

At Amsterdam airport, happy to have safe ground under her feet, and by now fully at ease in the company of the Chinese complement, she joined their special coach for the short drive into the city. It was midnight when the young men were dropped off at a seamen's hostel, all smiles and goodbyes, and my mother found herself stranded in a dimly-lit back street, with no provisions having been made to conduct her to a hotel for the night. Apart from two sparsely clad women loitering at a corner, and a single car cruising as for sightseeing, she found herself alone with her suitcase and without a shred of Dutch to her name. She was also exhausted, anxious for the comfort of a bed. Then she saw it: fifty yards down the road. A red light. A 'Hotel' sign. She blessed her luck and heaved her luggage to the welcome shelter.

Here, in reply to her request for a room, a heavy-weight type whom she took for a porter looked at the elderly lady and her modest attire as if he were hallucinating. Only when my mother explained her predicament in a medley of German and schoolgirl English did he hand her a key and, with a broad grin, pick up her suitcase. 'Mind you,' my mother would recall, 'the room was quite plain and the mattress rather worn out, but I was so tired that I fell asleep immediately and did not wake once.' Next morning, the same man brought her croissants and a steaming cup of chocolate, apologising for some 'commotion' during the night. Finally, a taxi took her to the station and on the penultimate leg of her journey home.

It says something for my mother's genteel upbringing, and her naivity as regards a certain profession, that she had no idea in what kind of hotel she had spent the night, nor that in certain districts of a city a red light indicates what in Germany is known as a *Stundenhotel* (or 'hotel-by-the-hour'), where 'guests' seldom stay longer than an hour and mattresses never stay firm for long.

I am glad to say that the last leg of my mother's journey passed without a hitch. No doubt she would have been mighty impatient to tell her friends what had befallen her on the journey home.

Civil Unrest

In July 1967, at the end of our second tour of the Colony, we lived through a period of civil unrest.

Following the Civil War in China, which had spawned the Cultural Revolution, radical elements believed to be on Peking's payroll tried to foment anti-British sentiments by inciting local Communist sympathisers to rioting. Posters proclaimed Hong Kong to be a 'capitalist blot' on the Chinese landscape; stones, and even poisonous

Anti-British posters on Kowloon buses: 'We will definitely win.
The British government in Hong Kong is deemed to be defeated.
Immediately release the arrested Chinese fellow citizens.'

109

snakes in open cartons, were thrown into trams and buses, and there were incidents in which hydrochloric acid was sprayed at police with children's water pistols. A few Europeans who had unwisely or unwittingly strayed into Mong Kok, one of Kowloon's most densely populated areas, were beaten up. Things got so bad that the Army schools were closed and families were advised not to venture outdoors despite temperatures roosting in the nineties. I could no longer take the children swimming, or allow them to play or ride their bikes in our close. Cooped up as we were in the house and the small walled backyard all day, it required maternal ingenuity to ward off frustration and tantrums.

At night, the eerie drone of helicopters cruising over British Army quarters and barracks, as they scanned roofs and streets with powerful searchlights, made for uneasy sleep, while during the day armoured cars patrolled the streets as if in wartime. There were no deliveries of milk, newspapers and groceries, and we had to rely on Aho to do the necessary shopping. Feeling like unwilling bit-players in a Peking-engineered tug of war, and suddenly unwelcome in a place in which we had grown temporary roots, we were now counting the days until we could finally turn our backs on what increasingly looked like an explosive situation.

Although our outward passage in 1961 had taken us through two frenzied storms which had brought home to us the power of the elements at sea, the experience had obviously not weaned us off another ocean sailing. For, when during the weeks of rioting we had to decide whether to return by air or on the P&O liner *Oronsay*, we chose the latter. But then, who would not have opted for a paid-for luxury holiday at sea with the chance of going ashore again in foreign ports? The fact that the 28,000-tonne ship was fitted with stabilisers and had air conditioning throughout made our decision even easier. Other incentives were the expected culinary delights, as well as an entertainment programme that would leave no time for boredom.

Communist elements were still making the streets unsafe when our packing cases arrived and with them new priorities that distracted the children and me from our involuntary incarceration.

I remember it was a scorching day when we got ready to vacate our flat and move into a Kowloon hotel to await the arrival of the Southampton-bound ship on which three first-class two-bunk outside cabins had been booked for us. And just as three years earlier at the end of our first 'tour', when we had had to pack up and crate all personal items for storage and account for every Army-issue spoon, cup, towel and bedsheet before flying back to the UK on inter-tour leave, we now had to say goodbye to what had been home for another three years, and which like the previous Army-allocated housing had come with all too plain, soulless furniture and in non-matching upholstery and curtain fabric. The frustrated home maker in me sighed, as I remembered my grandmother and mother's cosy, tastefully furnished flats – the mahogany and shiny rosewood furniture, beautifully draped lace curtains, Persian carpets ... Yet like every British Army wife I also realised that despite our regimented furnishings it also meant worry-free, low-rent living. Repairs, too, were no problem. If a piece of crockery broke, it was replaced; if a chair wobbled, the QM would send a joiner. For free.

The Quartermaster arrived dead on time, assisted by two corporals who scrutinised every corner for dust and meticulously counted and listed every item of Army property. With great zest, he wielded his pen, noting any damage or deficiency. At the end of the two-hour procedure, my husband wrote out a cheque for two chipped dinner plates, a missing fork and some scratches to play-room furniture. On the way out, the 'master of housing' smiled broadly. 'I see you're going to Berlin,' he said. 'Good place. Good beer. And I liked their sausages.'

A good place? Suddenly my mind opened up a mixed bag of memories: of the city in which I was born. At which at the tender age of ten my parents had divorced and – for whatever lukewarm reasons – I had been dispatched to Potsdam, to live in a children's home. Berlin, where in February 1945 – having only just made it back on an eastern refugee trek – I had experienced one of the heaviest Allied bombing raids which brought me uncomfortably close to death; where my grandmother had died from starvation and, in the wake of Hitler's last war effort, my 15-year-old cousin had ended his life in Russian gunfire, and his parents were shot dead at point-blank range by looting Russian soldiers. Berlin, where before my marriage my health had taken frequent, painful tumbles that had more than familiarised me with hospitals and operating theatres, and where only recently (after 22 years of waiting for Red Cross confirmation) my mother had her second husband and reluctant 50-year-old conscript declared 'dead', missing at the Eastern front and presumed to have either been killed by enemy action or have died in a Siberian prison camp.

But now my thoughts lit up. Had my children not been born in Berlin, and love, laughter and a new lightness of being taken the bitterness out of my mind? My mother, I reminded myself, would be delighted to have us living in the same city again, seeing her grandchildren growing up and her lone widowhood filled with family life. And, had the new Berlin, which had heaved itself out of the ashes of the War, not made its mark again on the European map of politics and economy? Yes, I thought, Berlin was a good posting. Even if I had yet again to live with G-Plan furniture and under the command of another Quartermaster!

My husband interrupted my musings. 'Time to go,' he said, as an Army driver arrived to take us to a hotel in Tsim Sha Tsui, a tourist area still largely unaffected by the rioting. 'Children, say "goodbye" to Aho.'

Visibly embarrassed by our demonstrations of gratitude and good wishes, and hiding her own emotions under a Chinese smile, she allowed me to hug her – an endearment perhaps not expected from a foreign 'Missie' and the wife of her 'Master', and thus not reciprocated. I felt I was losing more than a maidservant and nanny, yet not until much later would I come to appreciate Aho's loyalty, indeed her love for our children.

Clasping their plastic mini suitcases, each stuffed with Lego, Corgi cars, sketching or colouring material, a book, the latest copy of *The Beano* and whatever they had fancied to take along as a mute travelling companion, the children took their own leave of Aho. 'Will you come and visit us?' they asked, perhaps taking her smile for an answer. Small arms clasped her white apron, and a hint of sadness whisked across their faces like a storm-driven cloud. Then they raced towards the open door with the adaptability of the young who, not yet grasping the finality of some farewells, are already looking forward to all the momentous things they would soon see, hear and experience.

A last look at another brick-and-mortar repository of memories, a wave, then we were on our way.

At the hotel we were greeted by the news that embarkation would be delayed by a day or two. Halfway between Japan and Hong Kong a fire had apparently broken out in one of the ship's holds. To contain its spread it had become necessary to flood more than forty cabins and these would now require refurbishment. The traditional belief, superstition or myth came to my mind, as spun by old sea dogs from one generation to another, that a fire on board a ship augurs ill for its remaining passage. However, all we could do was to make the best of the delay.

On the last evening, after dark, we went onto the roof of the Ocean Terminal to look at the view across the harbour for the last time. It was a sight which I knew would stick in my memory, whatever future building developments might already be on the architects' drawing-boards.

We did not realise yet that we had left Dunbar Road just in time.

PART III

A JINXED HOMEWARD PASSAGE

The Evil Eye

A sun-drenched quayside, a rearguard of Chinese onlookers, British families bidding friends farewell, streamers fluttering lustily in the strong breeze, a Gurkha band musically accompanying passengers up the gangway. The *Queen Mary*, I thought, would not have

A musical send-off

SS *Oransay*

commanded a more impressive embarkation and send-off. It was late afternoon when to the strains of 'Rule, Britannia!' and the oompah of brass the *Oronsay* eased herself out of Hong Kong harbour. And now, minute by minute, familiar shores and towering landmarks were shrinking until sea mist began to shroud, then erase their contours, as the ship nosed her way into the choppy waters of the South China Sea.

A frisson of sadness rumbled through my pleasant anticipation of the passage ahead, for somehow I knew that I would never return and that I would have to take good care of my memories.

We had been one day at sea when the skies darkened, the wind rose sharply and white-crested waves began to slap the hull of the ship. A tropical storm was brewing, which before long, and despite the vessel's stabilisers, finally saw us meekly retire to our cabins on a diet of water biscuits and mint tea. Not unreasonably, the thought crossed my mind that there might be some truth in the sailors' lore that a fire on board puts a curse or an evil eye on the ship for the length of her passage. Subsequent events seemed, indeed, to bear out my conjecture.

We were approaching the Strait of Malacca when an elderly

passenger died and was buried at sea at the first light of dawn, before the first health-conscious joggers started on their deck rounds. Not much later there came the news that the riots in Hong Kong had reached a critical stage, and that an extremist had thrown an explosive device at officers' quarters in Kowloon. At the time, distanced as we were by now from events in the Colony, the news generated no more than speculations over pre-dinner drinks as to whether Mao's China – thirty years ahead of its eventual handover – was merely divining Hong Kong's political climate by cleverly playing its local puppets. 'It'll blow over,' said a middle-aged passenger whose bearing and clipped speech suggested senior Army officer or diplomatic status. 'We've dealt with similar situations before. Believe me, Mao wouldn't dare break the contract with Her Majesty's Government. He just likes to shake the status quo a little from time to time.' Everyone agreed, and over another whisky soda or G&T a retired colonial administrator related his own experience of local political pique. All this led me to reflect

Dunbar Road

119

that only a national disaster or some ground-shaking news from Westminster or Buckingham Palace could ever rattle British composure.

But then, in Singapore, we received a letter from our former next-door neighbour in Dunbar Road, telling us that a Chinese youth had tried to throw what was believed to be a hand-grenade through the living room window of our former first-floor flat. Badly aimed, though, from only a few yards underneath the window, the device had apparently exploded on impact with the bars, its force recoiling and seriously injuring the thrower.

'What good luck you left when you did,' wrote the mother-of-two. 'Fancy, if you and the children had been sitting by the window and the device had passed through the bars... All hell broke loose afterwards – police, the Army, the QM. They say the youth was caught running away, bleeding badly. All is quiet now. But, thank God, we're in for a UK posting next month.'

I had to force myself not to dwell on the 'What if...'. Anyway, by the time we went ashore in Colombo, the sea miles had already distanced me from the recent past.

Colombo

We docked in Colombo harbour after breakfast. The sun was well up in a porcelain sky and the temperature heating up like an oven. Flags were hanging limp, and the air was sighing for a breath of onshore wind. At the quayside a group of dancers performed their welcoming routine. Undeterred by what promised a scorching, stamina-demanding day, land-trippers set off in all directions.

We went straight into town and into the shambolic life of its main street. Having lived in orderly, British-managed Hong Kong, I was immediately struck by the rich tapestry of Colombo's foreignness. Ramshackle red buses and a few veteran taxis hooted their way through the crowd, whirling up bulbous clouds of dust

Colombo – High Street

and narrowly missing ox-drawn carts, tuk-tuks, cyclists, mangy dogs, water carriers, disoriented chickens and at least one member of the bovine family trotting blithely through the mêlée. Monks, robed in bright orange, formed beacons in this street chaos, while a hapless policeman on a raised platform vainly tried to impose right of way.

When the heat began to turn our sightseeing promenade into enforced exercise, and the buggy refused to skip over yet another bump in the unpaved road, a taxi ride took us past the shacks of the urban hinterland, grazing buffalos and a riot of flame trees to the Botanical Gardens and its verdant dome of shade. In this oasis hibiscus trees burst with crimson blossoms and smooth carpets of lawn and exotic flowers lined the public paths – a perfect refuge in which to restock on mental and physical energy.

An elephant and its keeper touted for custom and soon the children and I were heaved aloft onto rattan seats. Off we went at the animal's more than leisurely speed. Suddenly Donald squealed with delight when the creature loudly broke wind and dropped huge parcels of dung. 'Look, Mummy, what the elephant has done,'

Colombo Botanical Gardens

A snake charmer

he cried, his boisterous expression of amusement reaping amused smiles among the native onlookers.

A snake charmer brought the children into close contact with another specimen of the local fauna. Watching the handler piping his pet out of its basket, and holding it in his hand like a strand of rope, he invited the youngsters to touch it. However, only John felt brave enough to poke a finger at the vile-looking exhibit. Andrew only went through the motions and Donald shrank back visibly from touching, live, what he had only encountered in his comic books as wicked and poisonous.

The shadows were getting longer when we took refreshments on the airy veranda of a beachside hotel which did not deny its faded ex-colonial style. Sadly, time did not allow us to visit the hills of Candy and the region's famous tea plantations, nor the temple in which one of Buddah's teeth is allegedly enshrined. Guided excursions were not yet part of a P&O cruising programme at the time.

Back on board we learnt that a German measles epidemic had broken out, affecting many children and, worse, a few adults. Restrictions on movements were imposed and patients had to stay in their cabins for barrier nursing. To the dismay of the healthy children, the kindergarten and play areas were closed and all competitions cancelled. Not surprisingly, while doctors and nurses were kept on their toes, a quarantine feel reigned on deck and in the public rooms.

Once again I was left wondering whether there might be some truth in the mythical 'evil eye', and whether further incidents might jeopardise the vessel or its passengers. In the bar that night an elderly passenger in an ill-fitting dinner jacket, whose deep-tanned, weather-beaten face betrayed a life lived at sea or under a tropical sun, delivered his own views on the subject in a voice which did not invite arguments.

'Poppycock!' he blurted out. 'When I lived on Java... '

He was not short of listeners.

Singapore Revisited

When the ship tied up at the pier, the sun was struggling to penetrate the heat haze which blanched the city. Yet nothing would deter us from going ashore. Following an early rain shower, high humidity, combined with traffic fumes, was hanging lead-like over the streets. Predictably, it was not long before my husband – an early candidate for asthma – was gasping for air. 'We can't traipse around like this all day,' he wheezed and hailed a taxi. 'Let's go to the Sultanate of Jahore. They say there's a fabulous mosque, right in the middle of the jungle.'

The twenty-odd-mile drive took us through long stretches of untamed forest, past pockets of habitations and rubber estates. At one plantation we watched latex drop lazily from tapped trees into tin cups hung underneath each bleeding, bark-stripped incision, which instantly gave the word 'rubber' an uncomfortable connotation.

We also stopped at a cluster of box-shaped, grass-thatched huts built on stilts, where womanfolk received us with smiles and a torrent of Malay. Wearing voluminous head-dresses and gaily coloured robes, the women readily posed for photographs, their faces friendly and maternal as they forked their hands through our children's hair as if it were of an unknown texture. While the adults conducted a conversation of sorts in Malay, pidgin English and sign language, the brown-skinned children played football with the empty shell of a coconut, inviting ours to share their game.

When it was time to move on, we found Donald to be missing. With our shouts drowned in the dense undergrowth of the jungle, a search party went out. And now fear started creeping through my insides, all too keen to paint an ugly picture. Had our youngest been kidnapped? Had he encountered a wild animal?...

Suddenly there sounded a heavy plomp, like the drop of a dud bomb. A large coconut had fallen, had in fact been tossed, from a nearby tree which had grown at a freak angle, thus easing a climber's access to its crown. Seated high up, the thrower, our little escapee, now began to make his descent as from a steep rock, in the process grinning as if he had licked the proverbial cat's cream. His climbing prowess, first practised on the window bars of our Kowloon flats, gave early notice that as a young man and undergraduate no mountain peak would be safe from him. (As a member of the Glasgow University mountaineering team he would climb Mont Blanc, paying dearly for the feat with frostbite on his toes.) Now, at the completion of his first notable feat, the amused women let him keep the coconut as a souvenir. Proudly he clasped it under his arm. I forget what happened to it. Perhaps he drank the sweet milk or shared it with his brothers. He certainly did not take it home like a trophy.

The Sultanate of Jahore – mosque

I do not remember much of our visit to the Sultan's famous mosque. All that comes to mind are hazy images of sun-enhanced golden cupolas, decorative stonework, the intricacy of coloured tiles and the artistry of mosaic and faience. In the central courtyard, from which a door led to the inner sanctum, off-limits to 'infidels' and guarded by a mullah, there reigned a devout stillness which called for whispers and the light tread of stockinged feet.

Today I still regret that in those years I lacked the necessary curiosity and motivation to want to learn more about world religions and Eastern civilisations, more about the broad spectrum of history. At the time, history meant no more to me than what I remembered

Singapore Botanical Gardens

from my schooldays: European wars and dynasties, the cause and effect of revolutions; a chapter or two on Elizabeth I, Louis Quatorze, Napoleon, Abraham Lincoln and Peter the Great; volumes on Adolf Hilter's grand schemes for a phoenix-like rise of the Fatherland from the dictates of the Treaty of Versailles. Not until I was past middle age would I develop a keen interest in ancient and modern history, as well as in everything that has shaped the world as it is today.

In Singapore, under open skies and a broiling sun, we escaped once again to the Botanical Gardens, lazing around and watching monkeys gambolling on manicured lawns.

I wonder to what places of interest a guided tour would take us today, and how my travel notes would bulge with entries about the history, architecture, the different faiths and customs of indigenous people.

Now that age and infirmity deny me a chance to make up for areas of ignorance by study *in situ*, I am resigned to the fact that I shall never spend a night in a Siberian yurt, like Colin Thubron, never travel along the Silk Road with Paul Theroux, never experience Bill Bryson's small-town America. No longer will I go on safari in Africa, test my stamina in the Australian Outback or see brown bears emerging from hibernation in the Yukon. And what about walking down Fifth Avenue or strolling around the Lyceum where the great Aristotle is said to have composed his lofty thoughts?... Now that it is too late for globe-trotting and wide-eyed wonder, I have to be content with travellers cum explorers' erudite accounts as well as with televisual travelogues. I have become an armchair traveller, a passionate reader of books whose authors take me on their journeys like a silent companion.

Bombay

By the time we reached Bombay no further cases of measles had been reported and life on board was back to its usual hedonistic routine. I was looking forward to going ashore with the family, to getting a glimpse of the city and perhaps a whiff, a whisper, of India itself: the country long ruled by the British Raj and popularly associated at the time with Gandhi, maharajas, magi, beggars, holy men and sacred cows; with pilgrims bathing in the Ganges, funeral pyres, searing heat, dust and hot spices – a collage of observations and experiences recounted, or written about by expatriates, travellers and early traders. For many, also a country unforgettably evoked in Kipling's *Kim*.

However, things did not work out as scheduled. The ship had to drop anchor offshore due to a dockers' strike which was not expected to end before evening. Early-morning mist was shrouding the harbour and the city beyond in anonymity. Frustrated and impatient to set out on their 'Bombay-in-a-few-hours' sightseeing, passengers hugged the railings all day, waiting for the ship to berth. But not before sunset did we finally enter the harbour. Shore leave was extended until midnight, to allow the ship to load and unload freight and shore-goers to at least get a feel of the pulse of the city.

To our children's delight we adjourned bedtime for an hour and went ashore.

Immediately we were assailed by outstretched hands and the vociferous cries of vendors of carpets, jewellery and other native crafts. One swarthy character stuck a ring under my husband's nose. 'Ruby,' he cried, 'very cheap.'

'Only an idiot would buy anything in this light,' muttered my husband, shoving the man out of his way and urging his family to stay close together. With time at our heels, he hired a taxi and asked the driver to show us the sights of Bombay. 'Mahatma will do,' replied the owner of the vehicle which looked as if it had seen its heyday in the time of the last British viceroy.

Soon we were driving along palm-fringed avenues, past flagged and illuminated government buildings and colonial, Palladian-style mansions, all of which rose nobly behind smooth and verdant lawns. We were being shown, I felt, the city's official calling card. 'This is not the real Bombay,' I said to the driver. 'Please take us to the old parts of the city.'

As if he had been waiting to be redirected, the driver immediately spun the car around, and soon the less touristy quarters of the city opened up: narrow, filthy streets, hovels, stray dogs, beggars and feral children galore; streets reeking of poverty, dereliction, putrification and sewers. In one especially dirty-looking thoroughfare, the taxi, wrestling its way past steaming kitchens and market stalls, came to a sudden halt. 'Close up the windows!' urged the driver, but those at the back, where the children and I were sitting, would yank up only an inch or two, not enough to keep a pack of ragged child beggars from ambushing us. '*Baksheesh*,' they cried, faces unsmiling, urgency in their voices. Open hands shot through the windows, demanding their dues. When these were denied, the scene grew ugly. Dirty fingers now waved threateningly in front of my face, hands no longer begged but mounted an attack. Trying to touch the boys' hair, grasp our bare arms, hook onto our clothes. Their anger was intimating '*Baksheesh* or else'. Scared, our youngsters pressed close to me, while I fought off the invaders with one hand, and with the other vainly tried to wind up the window. By now the heat was closing in. Gasping for air and seeing our personal space seriously threatened, my husband finally parted with a few rupees, whereupon the young mob withdrew, to fight among themselves for a share of the alms. And now, as to a given signal, the obstacle ahead cleared and the taxi moved on. (To this day I

130

wonder whether the incident was just one of many beggar-friendly stops, and whether the window mechanisms on the rear seats of other taxis had been similarly 'disabled' to allow young beggars easy access.)

The driver now had another sightseeing 'treat' up his sleeve. Turning into a side street, in which a steady stream of males were sauntering along or sitting over a bowl of rice, our attention was drawn to long rows of first-floor windows, behind each of which a woman was seated, bathed in rose-tinted light and wearing a sari of striking colours. None of them moved, as if they were posing for a portrait. 'Bombay cage district,' explained the driver, 'always busy.'

Speechless I stared at the spectacle which broke new ground in my education. What would the children make of it? I wondered. Indeed, John, forever seeking an explanation for things he did not understand, promptly asked: 'Mummy, what are those ladies doing up there?' My husband tried to force back a grin, while I dug out a quick answer appropriate to the child's age and that of his siblings, one which precluded information on legalised or tolerated prostitution in a designated and controlled environment. 'They're showing off their beautiful clothes,' I replied, trying to keep a straight face. I am happy to say that my white lie was accepted without further probing into what to him and his brothers would have appeared as an exotic fashion show.

By the time we got back to the ship the children had fallen asleep. I felt we had seen of Bombay at night as much as any flying visit will grant: both antiseptic tourist views of the city and the reeking, teeming life of its backstreets. A mere glance at one of India's urban scenes – but not the real India.

Re-Routed

Back at sea, it was not long before passengers and crew went down with diarrhoea and vomiting, a mass outbreak which once again turned the *Oronsay* into a hospital ship. Tests revealed that the water taken on in Bombay was contaminated, most likely by the heavy monsoon rains which had earlier caused widespread flooding. For days, pale-faced passengers slouched around the promenade deck, taking in lungfuls of sea air, or lounged morosely in deckchairs.

We were halfway through the Arabian Sea on the way to the Gulf of Aden before pre-dinner 'happy hour' was back in full swing and five-course meals back on the menu. It was at this moment, however, that the Captain announced the re-routing of the

Pre-dinner cocktails – first class

ship. Owing to an escalation of the Arab-Israeli War, Egypt had closed the Canal to all foreign shipping for an indefinite period. Much to the delight of many passengers, ourselves included, the *Oronsay* was to set course around the Cape and up the west coast of Africa, calling on the way at Durban, Cape Town and Dakar. Our arrival at Southampton was expected to be delayed by the best part of one week. As the ship turned to sail south, all I could think of was that the detour and, ergo, the extension of our holiday was a chance to set foot on African soil. Surely, I reckoned, the ship would have shaken off its jinx by now and be back in the favour of the sea spirits. Plain sailing would lie ahead. And so, at last, it did.

Now bound for the Cape and the Southern Hemisphere, we briefly sailed along the coasts of Oman and the Yemen, their distant shores teasing the eye.

After lunch, once passengers had retired to their cabins for a siesta or were dozing in deckchairs, children safely packed off to the kindergarten for the 'quiet hour', I leaned against the ship's railing, training my sight on the shy contours of the coastline. I became aware of an acute flutter of déjà vu, as my inner eye crossed into the Empty Quarter, the Rub' al Khali, southern Arabia's vast sandy desert into which no European had ventured before the thirties. A novel I had recently read, set in this mind-boggling expanse two centuries ago, had brilliantly evoked the utter emptiness, remoteness and legendary cruelty of the barren landscape about the size of Western Europe. Its bloody history encompassed tribal warfare, exquisite torture and fiendish punishments besides other atrocities committed in the name of Allah, greed and honour. Although a work of fiction, the book's images of this wild, immense blot on the global map had fascinated me, and now it stretched before me, just a few sea miles away! My inner camera was clicking away, and my senses picked up the voices of the desert and the saffron-spiced wind, before an offshore heat haze veiled, then erased the outline of the coast as if to block further incursion. My mental journey into the Rub' al Khali had ended. However, the very dimensions of its emptiness would continue to intrigue me. I would become an avid reader of books recounting treks through the Empty Quarter or through any other mind and body-challenging desert on earth.

As the tinkling of cups and saucers called passengers to the English afternoon tea ritual, and the band struck up, the *Oronsay* veered sharply southward on course for Durban and the Cape.

A day later we entered equatorial waters. In glorious sunshine, and riding on an amicable Somalian current, the traditional 'Neptune's Baptism' of the children on board took place. On leave from his

Neptune's baptism. John in centre, Donald and Andrew far left.

bridge, the Captain formally opened the show, and the children – swimmers and non-swimmers – lined up at the seawater pool, besides which buckets of soft vanilla ice cream and an outsize spatula were waiting. There was a fairground atmosphere, heightened no doubt by stewards serving the audience free 'equatorial' cocktails to live music.

One by one the children stepped forward to subject themselves to the 'Baptism'. A member of the crew would cap each candidate with a large dollop of ice cream, which, quickly melting in the heat, ran down the child's face in rivulets, sweet manna for furiously licking tongues. Next, once a ship's officer had read out a few lines of a jingle, the youngster was told to jump or was gently shoved into the pool, where two crew members assisted the non-swimmers to survive the procedure, accompanied by hearty applause. Finally, having showered off the vanilla-scented pool water, and before being restored to parental care, each 'ducked' child received a certificate from the Captain. The sea god's pseudo-ritual had been duly observed.

No wonder the children did not request an ice-cream dessert at their high tea that day.

We were sailing through the Mozambique Channel, still enjoying hot sunshine and calm waters, when a children's fancy-dress competition was held. The Entertainment Officer produced a variety

Children's fancy dress party. Donald far left. Andrew next to him.

of material for mums to chose from and turn their youngsters into recognisable characters of their choice. With reputations for inventiveness and skill at stake, mothers went to work like professional costume fitters, foregoing games of bridge, visits to the hair salon and other recreational pursuits, while their darlings amused themselves in the kindergarten. I got busy with crêpe paper, coloured carton, scissors and paste, and rummaged our suitcases for some special accessories. John, the nine-year-old, fresh from reading *Treasure Island*, saw himself as Long John Silver, complete with a black eyepatch, coal-swarthened complexion and a stick poking out of his right trouser leg. Andrew, prompted by what he had read about the occupation of France during the war, went as a French Resistance fighter, wearing a beret and holding a plastic gun at the ready, while Donald in his red, 'ermine'-trimmed regal robe and golden paper crown made a fine king.

Strolling self-consciously down the catwalk to the applause of the spectators, sword-wielders, red Indians, Vikings, court jesters, angels, pirates and other fictional or mythical characters presented themselves for the scrutiny of the judges. Holding his head up high, and walking with the measured steps and the mien of a boy king, it came as no surprise when Donald was awarded first prize. No wonder that his mother sunned herself in the light of his win and the compliments of the Captain.

Durban

The weather had turned appreciably cooler by the time we reached Durban, the second largest port in South Africa and the city which has been described as Africa and India rolled into one. Sadly, I have but loose memories from our brief stay ashore, no more

A Durban tourist 'taxi'

139

View to the Valley of the Thousand Hills

than I would soon gather from Cape Town and Dakar. Once again time dictated the length and quality of our sightseeing, adding little to my existing knowledge about Africa and Africans. I admit I had not at that time heard of Robben Island or apartheid, or of countries

Zulu dancers

140

Zulu dancers

in the throes of independence. Perhaps I had been too preoccupied in the post-war period with my own struggle for survival in war-torn Germany, and later – in England in the late 1940s and 1950s – with carrying the heavy ballast of my country's recent history on my

The author posing for a photograph

A Zulu 'dwelling'

shoulders. Inevitably, my mental logbook of our fleeting African hours sadly records but a few splintered images.

Hotels lining the palm-fringed seafront bore witness to Durban being a popular holiday resort, attractive enough at first sight to stroll around. Yet, when a tourist coach begged for custom, the five of us soon found ourselves on the way to Zululand and the region of the Thousand Hills. The drive took us through Durban's Garden City, a well-heeled suburb featuring Dutch-style bungalows, well-kept lawns and gardens lush with tropical and subtropical blooms – a veritable feast for our eyes used as they had become to the dazzling yet monochrome seascape.

Zulu children

Somewhere in the densely wooded hills we visited a small Zulu settlement on a scrub-covered plateau. On arrival, bare-breasted, barefooted women lined up for a tribal dance and the likely gain of a few rands. Jumping up and down, their flimsy skirts flying, their breasts and voices riding on the monotonous rhythm of a drum, they commanded camera time. Shutters clicked like greedy tongues, while the dancers' faces displayed the weariness of performing animals.

At the end of the show, posing rigidly in line, they invited the tourists' children to join them for a photograph. But only Donald, our youngest, would come forward. With a rakish smile, and not at all intimidated by naked breasts, he took his place among them for the family album. Standing erect with the ease of natives, an earthenware vessel on their heads, the female troupe then coaxed the adults to pose with them. Spurred on by our offspring, I obliged. Next the children were invited with a gesture to pop into our hosts' thatched 'beehive' houses. Driven by the curiosity of the young, our boys slipped through the narrow opening of one, only to rush out again as if indeed stung by bees. Pinching their noses and crying 'uuuuuh', they commented none too discreetly on the smell inside. I'm afraid none of the adults opted to share this olfactory experience.

With the sun in descent, the temperature soon plunged and a chill wind swept across the hills. Not yet acclimatised to a colder clime, we shivered. And so did the semi-nude dancers, who now covered themselves up and went to offer the visitors handcrafted beaded necklaces for sale. A few rands changed hands and opened smiles, before our coach took us back to port.

Cape Town

Rounding the Cape of Good Hope, where the Atlantic meets the Indian Ocean and two south-running parallel currents meet head-on, the water grew quite turbulent – a freak oceanic behaviour, we were told, which had made this area the graveyard of many a ship in the past. The thought of wrecks lying deep down, perhaps right under the keel of the *Oronsay*, gave me an awed, yet delicious flutter of excitement, as did the realisation that Antarctica was now as close as I would ever come to it. Humpback whales sped us on our way towards the Atlantic, and our ship presently eased herself into Cape Town harbour.

Cape Town Harbour and Table Mountain

Donald climbing down from the 'Noon Gun'

It was winter in South Africa, which for us meant jumpers and anoraks. We went ashore in refulgent sunshine, buffeted by a cold northerly wind. Once again our time on land was all too brief, dictated by the ship's re-routing and unscheduled anchorage. I therefore remember little more than what my camera allowed me to snap: a handsome city hall, Dutch-style houses and a canon mounted on a pedestal in a large square, on which Donald soon sat astride (only a week later he would take up a similar position on one of the lions in London's Trafalgar Square). When told that the canon would fire a single shot at noon, as it did every day, and that the vibration would lift him high up into the air, our six-year-old looked at his father as if he'd been told that horses could fly. 'No, it won't,' he argued. 'It couldn't. There's no one to fire it. And, anyway, where's the gunpowder?' Taken aback, my husband was lost for words. He had obviously underrated the information youngsters can pick up from comics.

146

Satisfied with the effect his argument was having, Donald reluctantly dismounted the ancient monument.

A few minutes later – we had just left the square – a mighty boom rode across the city. The Noon Gun. My husband set his watch and shot a meaningful glance at his youngest son, who wrapped himself in silence. To this day I don't know from where the canon shot came. Certainly not from Donald's mock horse.

I recall a coach trip, passing vineyards, windmills and the architectural vestige of Dutch settlements. A photo-stop at a mile-long beach of white sand, free of sunbathers, swimmers and ball players, reminded me of 'our' Malaysian beach haven of six years ago. Later, my camera preserved for me the dramatic ocean views from Table Mountain and a the panoramic walk during which I explained to the children that the carpet of mauve heather which covered the hillside was a plant native to Scotland, where it enjoyed a similar climate. 'I'll show you when we get there,' I said. 'Won't be long now.'

'What else is there in Scotland?' came a young voice.

Table Mountain panoramic walk – the author showing her children heather

'Ooooch,' I said, 'to start with there are real cows and lots of real sheep; there are hills and rivers and streams...'

'Are there any fish in them?' asked Andrew, who seemed to have been born with an angler's ambition of hooking a prize-worthy fish.

'Plenty,' I replied.

Meanwhile, Donald, mindful of a picture showing a Scotsman in full Highland dress, asked the inevitable question. 'Do all Scotsmen wear frocks?'

'They call them kilts,' corrected John, 'and they don't wear anything underneath.'

'Is that true, Mum?' asked Donald.

I tried to keep a straight face. 'Well,' I said, 'as a woman I would not look under a Scotsman's kilt, would I?'

The children unanimously agreed. Now Donald addressed his father who was walking ahead of us. 'Is it true, Dad?' My husband had his reply ready. 'I don't know, son, and if I did I wouldn't tell you. It is a secret which Scotsmen never reveal.'

There followed a stunned silence in which I spoke of Highland games, caber-tossing, pipers and ceilidhs. 'Won't be long now,' I added.

'It won't be long now...' My simple statement suddenly reached out beyond Scotland and Berlin, to the fact that, indeed, it would not be long before, one after the other, the children would have to leave the parental nest to go to a British boarding school; not all that long either before, as young adults, they would set out to face the outside world and their own potential, when ultimately I would no longer be their sole beacon...

Under the penumbra of such thoughts I returned with the family to the ship, which presently weighed anchor.

*   *   *

Sailing close to the West African coast, once again crossing the Equator and basking in hot sunshine, we passed countries miles offshore, which stood in my mind as infamous slave ports and former colonies. Countries also known for their hellish temperatures, unpronounceable illnesses and often none-too friendly natives, and in which explorers and adventurers had risked, and frequently lost, their lives. Again my ignorance needled me. I knew no more of this vast 'Black Continent' than what had formed part of the class syllabus under National Socialism: the bitterly resented loss of Germany's colonies, the shameful chronicle of the slave trade, the Boer War... In more imaginative moments we had traced the course of the Nile, seen ourselves riding on camel-back through the Sahara Desert and shuddered at grisly accounts of local cannibalism...

I knew I would have to update my knowledge on Africa. Soon. Sometime.

Dakar to Southampton

Temperatures were now picking up fast, while clear skies and calm waters came as a premium. With just one more port and a brief amble ashore still to come, and with the sea miles to Southampton ever decreasing, every hour on board now seemed precious.

Dakar – harbour 'market'

Street market

We docked in Dakar at midday. The sun stood high in a bleached
sky and it was very hot. The ship anchored along a vibrant dockside
market, a teeming kaleidoscopic set-piece worthy of more than one
photo snap. Women shoppers wore elegantly draped gowns and
head-dresses in vivid colours and moved gracefully among the
traders as if giving a lesson in deportment.

With no idea of where to go, we wandered off into town. Here,
walking along the high street, I was similarly impressed by the
strikingly robed Senegalese women strolling down the *Rue*, tall
and erect, each a potential model for a fashion magazine. Indeed,
the very height of the local people and the ebony colour of their
skin – something I had never come across before – made them an
instant object of interest.

We made it to a beautiful mosque, but were not allowed more

Dakar Mosque

than a glimpse into its inner courtyard; we stopped at the President's abode, which with its playful architecture resembled a French château. It was guarded by massive wrought-iron gates and two armed sentries who looked as if they were on lease from Buckingham Palace. No objections were raised when, with the children in the foreground, I focused my camera on the presidential guardians.

In all, a flying visit, a mere picture-postcard stop. Sights flitting past too quickly to be framed, colours dissolving into monochrome too soon.

Back at sea – the children happily engaged in the supervised play area, my husband caressing a cold beer – I stood on deck watching the Senegalese coastline disappear like a mirage. Yet soon a new panorama opened up in my mind: West Berlin, our next posting, the city whose Western image was of an 'Island in a

153

Children outside President's Palace

Red Sea', but which Moscow and the DDR (the Deutsche Demokratische Republik, or East Germany), were labelling as 'a carbuncle on the Zone of Communism'. However, there now rose the cheery prospect of snow in winter, which would enable the children to go sledging and snowballing and even skiing on the Teufelsberg. There would be *Leberwurst* (liver sausage), crisp *Brötchen* (rolls) and delicious *Käsekuchen* (cheesecakes), and visits to the opera, theatre and philharmonic concerts; there would be lilac, tulips and catkins in spring, roses in summer and chrysanthemums in autumn; and once again the boys' beloved grandmother would be close to family life. At Christmas, presents would be lying under a 'real' pine tree; and on Easter Sunday the children would hunt for eggs in the garden. And – oh, what a comforting thought! – there would be no cockroaches swarming in the kitchen or flying through the window; no rats would be found splashing about in the toilet; and snakes, monkeys and tigers would be safely confined

154

to the zoo. With those soothing thoughts in mind I dressed up for the last formal evening on board.

By the time we had reached the Bay of Biscay, the weather had turned cooler and storm clouds appeared. We were not allowed to forget that we had entered the Northern Hemisphere and that October was waiting in the wings. True enough, we disembarked in Southampton in pouring rain and suffering from bad colds. But then, Scotland beckoned, and so did Berlin – years which I was determined to make as happy and fulfilled as possible. If only because it wouldn't be all that long now before...

First stop London, Trafalgar Square

155

EPILOGUE

We spent one week in Scotland, where against all expectations not a drop of rain fell, the sun shone in a mock Mediterranean sky, and young autumn winds no more than brushed our cheeks; a week in which our eyes wallowed in the deep green of meadows, pink heather-clad hills and the first tints of autumn, and which held all the pleasures of boating, hill-walking and fishing by a stream. We ate Scottish beef, fresh salmon and home-baked blueberry tarts. And how we relished the, oh, so potable water! As an avid tea drinker, I enthused about every freshly brewed pot of tea, while for my husband, who had grown up in Paisley, a beer or two in the local pub must have felt like a homecoming.

Travelling around in a hired car gave the children a chance to update their pictorial images of sheep, cattle, red deer and jumping fish. However, on the banks of Loch Ness they looked in vain for the 'monster' or any suspicious movement of the deep water that might have pointed to the existence of the legendary creature. Neither did curiosity score at a ceilidh in a Highland Hotel, where we did not allow them to investigate whether the male dancers were in fact...

Our short Scottish holiday was also admirably suited to re-adjusting physically and mentally to *terra firma* and the advent of everyday realities. But whatever lay ahead, I knew that our life in Hong Kong, as well as the outward and home-bound passage, would forever hold a privileged, accessible place in the vast rich archive of my life's memories.

Copies of the following books may be obtained from

6 Hog Green
Elham
Canterbury
Kent
CT4 6TU

The Naked Years, p.b., £7.95 inc. p.p. (UK)
The Alien Years, h.b., £10.99 inc. p.p. (UK)
The Deluge, p.b., £6.95 inc. p.p. (UK)
The Quarry, p.b., £10.99 inc. p.p. (UK)
Reflections (Poetry), £4.50 inc. p.p. (UK)

Cheques to be made out to Marianne MacKinnon